100 METHODS FOR TOTAL QUALITY MANAGEMENT

100 METHODS FOR TOTAL QUALITY MANAGEMENT

Gopal K. Kanji
and
Mike Asher

Sage Publications
London • Thousand Oaks • New Delhi

First published 1996

SAGE Publications Ltd
6 Bonhill Street
London EC2A 4PU

SAGE Publications Inc
2455 Teller Road
Thousand Oaks, California 91320

Sage Publications India Pvt Ltd
32 M-Block Market
Greater Kailash – I
New Delhi 110 048

British Library Cataloguing in Publication data

A catalogue record for this book is available from the British Library

ISBN 0 8039 7746 8
ISBN 0 8039 7747 6 (pbk)

Library of Congress catalog record available

Typeset by Photoprint, Torquay, Devon
Printed in Great Britain at the University Press, Cambridge

CONTENTS

PREFACE

An essential part of the development of a total quality management (TQM) process should be the education and training of everyone in the organization. The main objective should be to provide information on the principles and philosophy of TQM and training in the methods to help the organization implement total quality management in a systematic way. One of the main purposes of this book is to help all employees to understand the proper use of the total quality management methods required for the achievement of their organization's quality goals. It will also provide the educators and practitioners in this area with a comprehensive set of TQM methods.

Total quality management encompasses certain basic principles. To implement and practise these principles, it is necessary to understand the working of various methods of total quality management. These methods are classified in this book within four categories:

Management methods: for example, Deming wheel (Method 10).
Analytical methods: for example, failure mode and effect analysis (Method 37).
Idea generation: for example, brainstorming (Method 51).
Data collection, analysis and display: for example, tally charts (Method 96), histograms (Method 78) and pie chart (Method 88), respectively.

A list of methods, by category, is given on p. 10; an alphabetical list of *all* methods (with a brief description of their purpose or use) is given on p. 13.

Within each category, each TQM method is explained simply under the following headings:

- purpose
- when to use
- how to use
- benefits
- example

When put into practice, appropriate quality methods can rapidly give rise to quality improvement. Choosing the right methods for the development of a TQM process is one of the vital roles of management and the degree of success obtained will depend upon managerial skill. The total quality management process is complex and the use of some of these methods requires careful consideration and clear understanding.

UNDERSTANDING TOTAL QUALITY MANAGEMENT

Total quality management principles

To understand the process of total quality management (TQM), we will follow Kanji and Asher (1993) where all work is seen as 'process' and total quality management is a continuous process of improvement for individuals, groups of people and whole organizations. What makes total quality management different from other management processes is the concentrated focus on continuous improvement. Total quality management is not a quick management fix; it is about changing the way things are done within the organization's lifetime. To improve the process, therefore, people must know what to do, how to do it, have the right methods to do it, and be able to measure the improvement of the process and the current level of achievement.

Total quality management encompasses a set of four principles and eight core concepts. The four guiding principles are:

- delight the customer
- management by fact
- people-based management
- continuous improvement

Each of the principles can be used to drive the improvement process. However, to achieve this, each principle is expressed with the help of two core concepts to make the principle workable. The eight core concepts are given in Table 1.

Delight the customer

This focuses on external customers and asks 'What would delight them?' This implies a real need to understand the product or service, agree requirements and fulfil them. 'Delight' means being best at what really

Table 1   *Principles and core concepts of TQM*

Principles	Core concepts
Delight the customer	Customer satisfaction
	Internal customers are real
Management by fact	All work is process
	Measurement
People-based management	Teamwork
	People make quality
Continuous improvement	Continuous improvement cycle
	Prevention

matters most to the customer and this can change over time. Being in touch with these changes and *always* satisfying the customer are an integral part of total quality management.

Management by fact

Knowing the current quality standards of the product or service in your customer's hands is the first stage of being able to improve. You can only measure your improvement if you know the base you are starting from. Having the facts necessary to manage the business at all levels, and giving that information to everyone so that decisions are based upon fact, are an essential aspect of continuous improvement.

People-based management

If people understand what to do, how to do it and obtain feedback on their performance, they can be encouraged to take responsibility for the quality of their own work. The more people feel involved, the greater will be their commitment to customer satisfaction. Systems, standards and technology themselves will not provide quality. The role of people is extremely important in the continuous improvement of quality within an organization.

Continuous improvement

Total quality management is not a short-term activity that will finish when a set target has been achieved. It is not a programme or a project. It is a management process that recognizes that, however much we may improve, our competitors will continue to improve and our customers will expect more from us. Here, continuous improvement is an incremental change and not a major breakthrough, which should be the aim of all who wish to undertake the total quality management journey.

Core concepts for improvement

Each of the eight core concepts given in Table 1 can be used to drive the process of continuous improvement and to develop a framework for quality improvement over many years.

Customer satisfaction

Many companies, when they start the quality journey, become very introverted and deal with their own internal problems, neglecting their external customers. A better way is for companies to use their customers to learn what is important to them and then measure their own performance against customer expectation. Asking your customers to set customer satisfaction goals is a clear sign of an outward looking company.

To fulfil customer satisfaction, Federal Express, an American company, surveyed their customers to identify the top ten causes of aggravation. The aggravation points were weighted according to customer views of how important these were. A complete check was made of all occurrences and a

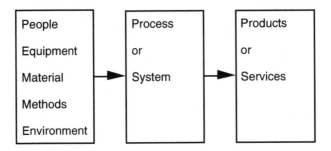

Figure 1   *Process*

weekly satisfaction index compiled. This allowed the company to keep a weekly monitor of customer satisfaction as measured by the customer.

Internal customers are real

Kanji and Asher's (1993) definition of quality – 'satisfying agreed customers' requirements' – relates to internal customers as well external ones. Many people also refer to the customer–supplier chain. We believe that it is necessary to achieve successful internal working relations in order to satisfy the needs of the external customer.

Whether you are supplying products or a service, the people you supply internally are as real as your external customers. They also require speed, efficiency or accurate measurement, but achieving a quality service between internal customers can sometimes be time-consuming. One way to deal with this is to assess poor quality in financial terms. Measuring the actual cost of poor quality, and the way that amount is made up, can provide an impetus for management to follow the quality improvement path. In this way, you can use the idea of the internal customer as a focus for improvement.

All work is process

Another possible focus for improvement is that of business processes. A process is a combination of methods, materials, manpower and machines (see Figure 1) that, taken together, produce a product or service. All processes contain inherent variability and one approach to quality improvement is progressively to reduce variation. This can be done, first, by removing variation due to special causes and, secondly, by driving down the common cause of variation, thus bringing the process under control and them improving its capability.

Measurement

This core concept of total quality management suggests that, in order to improve, we must first of all measure how we are doing at present. By measuring our present situation, we can focus both internal customer satisfaction and external customers' requirements. Internal quality measurement of production might include:

- breach of promise
- performance to standard
- reject level
- accidents
- process in control
- yield/scrap
- time cost due to non-available raw material
- number of changes to works order
- cost of quality

Teamwork

Teamwork can provide a real opportunity for people to work together to achieve quality improvement. People who work on their own or in a small group often have a picture of their organization and the work that it does which is very compartmentalized. They are often unfamiliar with the work that is done even by people who work quite near to them: as a result they are unaware of the consequences of poor quality in the work they themselves do.

Bringing people together in teams, with the common goal of quality improvement, aids communication between departmental or functional activities. Teamwork slowly breaks down the communication barriers and acts as a platform for change. Communication is part of the cement that holds together the bricks of the total quality management process supporting the principle of people-based management.

To communicate properly, it is necessary to focus on the receiver of the message. Communication is very much a two-way process. Managers often talk about the 'middle management sponge' into which information seems to go but out of which no information comes. Part of the problem is a lack of focus on the needs of those receiving the information. Figure 2 depicts a company with poor communication. For successful communication, you need to build credibility into the message and in the person giving the message. Anything that detracts from this does damage to both.

Teamwork also enables a group of people to work as a task force, looking at cross-functional problems, or as an action team, solving local problems, in order to identify and adopt new ways of doing things.

People make quality

Most of the quality problems within an organization are not normally within the control of the individual employee. As many as 80 per cent of these problems are caused by the way the company is organized and managed. The system often gets in the way of employees who are trying to do a good job. In such a situation it is difficult to solve the problem by simply telling the employees to do better. In these circumstances employee

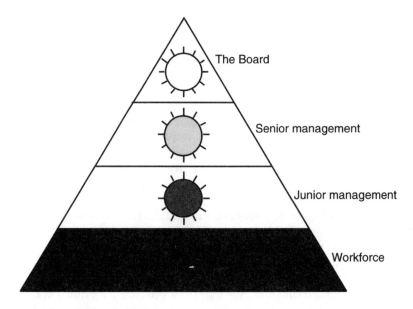

Figure 2 *Poor communication in an organization*

motivation alone cannot work. It requires real practical efforts on the part of managers to remove the barriers to quality improvement.

The role of managers within an organization is to ensure that everything necessary is in place to allow people to make quality. This, in turn, begins to create the environment where people are willing to take responsibility for the quality of their own work. Releasing the talents of everyone within the organization in this way can create a culture for quality improvement.

Continuous improvement cycle

The continuous cycle of establishing customers' requirements, meeting these requirements, measuring success and keeping on improving can be used both externally and internally to fuel the engine of continuous improvement. By continually checking customer requirements, a company can keep finding areas in which improvements can be made. This continual supply of opportunities can be used to keep quality improvement plans up to date and to reinforce the idea that the total quality journey is never-ending.

Prevention

This concept is central to total quality management and provides a positive approach to achieving continuous improvement. Prevention means seeking to ensure that failures will not occur. The continual process of removing the problems and failures out of the system will create a culture of continuous improvement.

There are several methods which are widely used for this purpose. Failure mode and effect analysis (Method 37) is a well-known method associated with both design and process analysis.

Pyramid model and leadership

From the outset, the total quality management approach has the vision that concentrated management action can improve the quality of service or products of an organization, at a very competitive cost, satisfying customers' needs and increasing market share. This increased market share will be stable because it has been earned with the help of solid customer goodwill and not by gimmicky advertising.

Kanji and Asher (1993) suggested a model which illustrates the principles of TQM as a pyramid. The base of the pyramid is occupied by the four principles of TQM and two core concepts correspond to each side of the pyramid. Although in Kanji and Asher's model the leadership of top management is central to the creation of a TQM organization, this is not emphasized in their diagram. We therefore produce a modified version of the pyramid model of TQM (see Figure 3) by simply extending the base of the pyramid. Here the organization has to be guided through the TQM principles and core concepts by top management leadership.

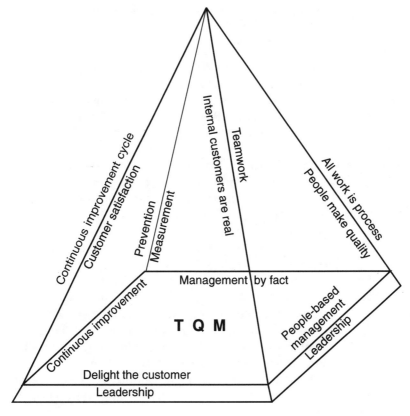

Figure 3   *Pyramid model of TQM*
Source: Kanji and Asher, 1993

THE ROLE OF TQM METHODS

Total quality management can be implemented by putting into practice suitable TQM methods. However, adopting the right kind of method is one of the most important jobs of senior management and the degree of success obtained will depend on their knowledge and understanding of these methods. TQM methods are unlikely to be useful if not used properly.

When TQM is implemented in an organization, it invariably starts with a simple procedure: the setting up of teams to solve particular problems. However, total quality management deals with quality culture, which is all about culture change based on a desire to satisfy the customer and eliminate existing problems permanently.

Education and training are key factors in total quality management, including the process of learning TQM methods. If teams start to look at quality management problems without proper training they will lose their way and become disheartened. If the quality problem is not identified accurately and the TQM method selected for solution based only on data analysis, then the problem will not be eliminated forever. In addition, the quality improvement process needs to be managed by an effective leader to ensure that proper implementation is achieved. By applying TQM methods properly and not fluctuating from one step to another before completion, the quality team will have a much greater chance of completing the task successfully.

The problem-solving process is a natural and logical sequence for overcoming quality problems and improving the standard of decision-making. It is also a guide for identifying which total quality management methods to be applied. Problems, no matter what their size or complexity, can best be solved by proceeding through a sequence of steps. This ensures that everything possible will be done by applying the available TQM methods in the most effective manner. It also gives the opportunity to consider a number of options and to select the best solutions.

Many quality problems, on the surface, appear to be simple to solve, and it is easy to leap to the first available solution. However, in the long term, for many problems it is unlikely that the best solutions will be found in this easy way. It is also possible that some side-effects will be generated, causing problems in other areas.

In total quality management all work is a process and the problem-solving process is a continuous cycle of opening your mind to a wide range of possible solutions and then deciding on the most feasible option. It is this continuous approach and the narrowing of the options that makes the TQM process so powerful.

The basic role of TQM methods in problem-solving for quality improvement is to help meet customer requirements. The methods also help to generate possible root causes and potential solutions, and to use data and information to select the best options for managing quality. To implement total quality management, it will be necessary to apply the methods in every aspect of business life.

LIST OF METHODS (BY CATEGORY)

Management methods

Analytical methods

Idea generation

Data collection analysis and display

PURPOSE OF METHODS (ALPHABETICAL LIST)

	Method	Page
Acceptable quality level (AQL) To provide a structure of sampling plans, risks and inspection strategies to ensure that the customer receives the quality that the supplier has contracted to deliver.	1	20
Affinity diagram To organize large amounts of data in groups according to some form of natural affinity.	2	23
Arrow diagram To show the time required for solving a problem and which items can be done in parallel.	3	25
Bar charts To display discrete data collected by checksheets so that patterns can be discovered.	68	154
Basic statistics The mean, median, mode, range and standard deviation are ways of summarizing and describing large volumes of data. The first three are measures of location, the last two are measures of spread.	69	156
Benchmarking To identify and fill gaps in performance by putting in place best practice, thereby establishing superior performance.	4	27
Box and whisker plots To provide a simple way of drawing the basic shape of the distribution of a set of data.	70	159
Brainstorming To generate as many ideas as possible without assessing their value.	51	123
Brainwriting To generate as many ideas as possible.	52	125
Breaking set To overcome blocks in thinking by generating new ideas. It is particularly useful in prompting a group to be more receptive to new suggestions.	53	127
Buzz groups A way of getting the immediate reaction of a group to a new idea or problem.	54	129
Cause and effect analysis To examine effects or problems to find out the possible causes and to point out possible areas where data can be collected.	32	79
C chart To identify when the number of defects in a sample of constant size is changing over time.	71	161
Checksheets To collect data when the number of times a defect or value occurs is important.	72	164
Concentration diagrams To collect data when the location of a defect or problem is important.	73	166
Consensus reaching To give a team a methodical way of examining alternatives to reach a collective conclusion which all team members can accept.	5	30

Contingency planning   To avoid 'firefighting' and waste of resources by planning for contingencies in the completion of a project.   6   32

Cost-benefit analysis   To estimate the real cost and benefits of a project under consideration.   7   33

Criteria Testing   To evaluate and compare alternative solutions to a problem by rating them against a list of criteria.   8   35

Critical path analysis   A project planning technique which separates the work to be done into discrete elements, allowing the key elements that affect the overall project to be identified.   33   81

Customers' contingency table   To understand the needs of both internal and external customers for the fulfilment of customer satisfaction.   9   37

Cusum chart   To identify when the mean value is changing over time.   74   168

Deming wheel (PDCA)   A management concept to satisfy the quality requirements of the customer by using the cycle: plan, do, check and action.   10   39

Departmental cost of quality   To provide a financial measure of the quality performance of an organization.   34   85

Departmental purpose analysis (DPA)   To review the internal customer–supplier relationship.   11   41

Domainal mapping   To assist in the identification of internal customers and their needs.   35   87

Dot plots   A simple graphic device which presents observations as dots on a horizontal scale.   75   171

Error proofing (pokayoke)   To design an operation in such a way that specific errors are prevented from causing major problems to the customer.   12   43

Evolutionary operation (EVOP)   A sequential experimental procedure for collecting information during on-line production to improve a process without disturbing output.   36   89

Failure mode and effect analysis (FMEA)   To assist in the foolproofing of a design or a process.   37   91

Fault tree analysis   To perform a quantitative as well as qualitative analysis of a complex system.   38   96

Flowcharts   To generate a picture of how work gets done by linking together all the steps taken in a process.   76   173

Force analysis   To identify external and internal forces at work when developing a contingency plan.   13   44

Force field analysis   Allows you to identify those forces that both help and hinder you in closing the gap between where you are now and where you want to be.   39   98

Gannt charts   For planning the steps necessary to implement quality improvement.   14   46

Geometric moving average   To identify trends in small changes in the process mean. The geometric moving average is sometimes called the exponentially weighted moving average (EWMA).   77   175

Histograms   To display continuous data collected by checksheets so that any patterns can be discovered.   78   177

Hoshin kanri (quality policy deployment)   To delight the customer through the manufacturing and servicing process by implementing the quality goals of the organization.   79   182

Idea writing   To bring all participants into groupwork.   55   130

Imagineering   To assist a company to identify areas of opportunity by concentrating on the ideal outcome then working back from it.   56   132

Improve internal process (IIP) plan   To provide the structure to develop work plan details for a task using various factors, such as measurables, responsible resources, times and previous task owners.   57   134

Is/is not matrix   To identify patterns in observed characteristics by a structured form of stratification.   80   184

ISO 9000   To demonstrate to yourself, your customers and an independent assessment body that you have an effective quality management system in place.   15   48

Just in time (JIT)   To deliver the raw materials or components to the production line to arrive just in time when they are needed.   16   50

Kaizen   A Japanese term meaning 'change for the better', the concept implies a continuous improvement in all company functions at all levels.   17   51

Lateral thinking   A way of transferring from one frame of reference to another, enabling you to break down barriers which inhibit creative thought.   58   136

List reduction   To reduce a list of ideas to one of manageable size.   59   138

Matrix data analysis   To provide a picture of numerical data from a matrix diagram in an efficient way.   81   186

Matrix diagram   To provide information about the relationship and importance of task and method elements of the subject.   82   188

Mind mapping   A way of generating and recording ideas individually rather than in a group. Mind mapping makes use of word associations, encouraging you to follow your own thought patterns, wherever they lead. It also provides a written record of the ideas generated.

Minute analysis To estimate the survival period of a particular product unit under certain conditions, using a simulated experimental environment. 40 101

Morphological forced connections To generate new ideas or ways of approaching problems. It combines lists of attributes and forces new connections between them, so triggering new options. 61 142

Moving average To identify trends in data when short-term variation or cyclical patterns are confusing the longer-term picture. 83 190

Multi-vari charts To show the dispersion in a process over the short and long term, using a graphic control chart. 84 192

Multi-voting To select the most popular or important items from a list. 62 144

Mystery shopping A technique involving looking at your business from the outside and measuring the efficiency of your own key processes from the customer's viewpoint. 18 52

Nominal group technique A way of generating ideas from a group and identifying the level of support within the group for those ideas. 63 145

NP **chart** To identify when the number of defective items in a sample of constant size is changing over time. 85 194

Objective ranking Helps to place your current activity in perspective and enable you to understand the purpose of your efforts. 19 54

Opportunity analysis Offers the opportunity to evaluate quickly a long list of options against desired goals and available resources. 64 147

Paired comparisons To help a group to quantify the preferences of its members. 41 103

Parameter design To determine which factors are important in the manufacturing process and to find the optimum set of working conditions. 42 105

Pareto analysis To separate the most important causes of a problem from the many trivial. Also, to identify the most important problems for a team to work on. 20 56

Paynter charts To display information over time in a way that allows changes in patterns of failure to be discovered. Paynter charts will show when one failure

mode takes over from another in terms of importance
or when the overall failure rate is changing over time.

P chart   To identify when the percentage of defective   87   199
items in a sample of variable size is changing over
time.

Pie charts   A way of pictorially representing data, pie   88   202
charts are an effective means of showing the relative
size of the individual parts to the total.

Potential problem analysis (PPA)   To examine plans   21   59
to identify what can go wrong with them, so that
preventive action can be taken.

Problem prevention plan   To anticipate what can go   22   61
wrong and plan to prevent problems.

Process analysis   Enables a group to look for   89   204
opportunities to improve processes. It can also be used
to identify standards and measures for critical parts of
processes.

Process capability   To demonstrate whether a process   90   208
is capable of meeting a specification and to calculate an
index to show this capability.

Process cost of quality   To provide a financial measure   43   107
of the quality performance of an organization.

Process decision programme chart   To focus on   23   63
possible sequences to help lead to a desirable result
and contingency planning.

Programme evaluation and review (PER)   24   65
technique   To establish a planning technique for
complex and multi-level projects.

Quality circles   A special type of small group activity   25   67
which forms a vehicle for the development of
individuals.

Quality function deployment (QFD)   A technique or   26   69
discipline for optimizing the process of developing
and producing new products on the basis of customer
need.

Relation diagram   To illustrate the relationship   27   72
between problems and ideas in complex situations. Also
to identify meaningful categories from a mass of ideas
when relationships are difficult to determine.

Reliability   To find the cause of failures and try   44   110
to eliminate them and to reduce the effects or
consequences of failure.

Rich pictures   To allow a group to capture all ideas   65   149
developed, without judgement or analysis, in a pictorial
form that allows the strength of the ideas to be
recorded.

Robust design (off-line quality control)   To achieve   45   112
the proper functioning of a component even when
affected by interfering factors, whether external,
internal or manufacturing variation.

Sampling   A method by which a small number of   91   210
items (the sample) is drawn from a larger number of
items (the population) in order to draw a conclusion
about the population based upon information from the
sample.

Scatter diagrams   To allow the relationship between   92   211
cause and effect to be established.

Snowballing   Sometimes called 'pyramiding', snowballing   66   151
is a technique for gathering information or ideas.

Solution effect analysis   To examine solutions to   46   113
problems to find out whether there are any detrimental
consequences and to plan the implementation of the
solution.

Spider web diagrams   To show performance against a   93   214
target when several criteria are being set.

Statistical process control (SPC)   To identify when   94   216
processes are changing over time.

Stem and leaf diagram   To present raw data and to   95   219
show their distribution visually.

Stratification   To assist in the definition of a problem   47   115
by identifying where it does and does not occur.

Suggestion schemes   To generate ideas for   67   153
improvement.

System design   To apply special scientific and   48   117
engineering knowledge to produce a basic functional
prototype model, having surveyed the relevant technology,
manufacturing environment and customer need.

Taguchi methods   A technique for the optimization of   49   119
products or processes, Taguchi involves a two-stage
experimental design that gives the benefits of
robustness and efficiency with the minimum number of
experiments.

Tally charts   To collect data when the value of a   96   221
defect or problem is important.

Teamwork   To organize activity which requires a   28   74
number of people to collaborate and work together for
a common goal.

Tolerance design   To find out by experiment where   50   122
the variability in a process (product) occurs and where
adjustments can be made.

Total productive maintenance   To help a process   29   75
which aims at making the most effective and efficient
use of existing production structures.

Tree diagrams   To identify the tasks and methods   97   223
needed to solve a problem and reach a goal.

U chart   To identify when the number of defects in a   98   225
sample of variable size is changing over time.

Why–how charting   When thinking in both abstract   30   77
and concrete terms, and needing to move between the
two, why–how charting enables a goal to be translated
into action.

X moving range (X-MR) chart   To identify when a   99   228
value is changing over time.

$\bar{X}$-R chart   To identify when the mean value or range   100   231
in a sample of constant size is changing over time.

Zero defects   To allow teams to experience the success   31   78
involved in meeting ever more demanding targets
without demotivating them by not achieving absolute
success at once.

MANAGEMENT METHODS

Method 1   Acceptable quality level (AQL)

Purpose

To provide a structure of sampling plans, risks and inspection strategies to ensure that the customer receives the quality that the supplier has contracted to deliver.

When to use

When sampling by attributes, so that each item inspected is classified as acceptable or unacceptable. AQL can be used for 'defective units', where the *whole* unit is classified as defective (e.g. incorrect forms or faulty bottles); or for 'defects', (e.g. errors on invoices or marks on paintwork).

How to use

Before any batch of work is sampled, it is essential to have certain specified information about the quality standards to be met, together with background information about the particular batch of work to be sampled. *Specific* information is:

1   The agreed acceptable quality level (AQL). This is defined as the worst quality which can be considered acceptable as the average 'per cent defectives' or 'defects per 100 units' of a process. AQLs are agreed between the supplier and external customer or between internal suppliers and customers. AQLs range from 0.0100 to 1,000 defects per 1,000 units and are given in BS 6001.

2   The inspection level. This allows some latitude in sample sizes. There are three inspection levels: normal; tightened; and reduced. An AQL is the borderline between acceptable and unacceptable quality. When an AQL has been agreed, the ideal situation is to have all batches better than the AQL accepted and all those worse rejected. Since this is impossible, AQLs use something called an 'operating characteristic curve' which tells you the risks that you are taking and effectively allows the level of risk to be chosen to reflect your knowledge of the current situation and what is important to you.

  • *Normal inspection* is designed to protect the supplier against a high level of rejection. In effect, the supplier is given the benefit of any doubt. The customer receives protection from a set of rules that allow switching to 'tightened inspection' when the supplier's performance is shown to have become less satisfactory.

- *Tightened inspection* makes it less likely that a faulty batch will be passed.
- *Reduced inspection* occurs when the supplier's performance has consistently been better than the AQL agreed.
- *BS 6001* gives rules for switching from one inspection level to another and the consequences of this.

3 Knowledge of whether defective units or defects are being inspected for.

   Background information is:

4 What is the size of the batch to be inspected?
5 Is the batch

- part of a series of batches which have already been inspected?
- the first batch of a new series?
- a 'one-off' or isolated batch?

6 The most advantageous method of sampling:

- *Single sampling*: a single sample of a given size is taken and a decision made to accept, reject, or sample the whole batch if more than a given number of defects is found.
- *Double sampling*: a sample is taken of a smaller size than the single sample and then a decision is taken to accept, reject or take a second sample.
- *Multiple sampling*: an extention of double sampling, allowing up to seven samples to be taken before a decision is made.
- *Sequential sampling*: no fixed sample size; the samples are accumulated until enough information is available to make a decision.

Benefits

AQL and BS 6001 give a set of rules on acceptance and rejection of samples, based upon the sample size and number of defects found in the sample, that can be mutually agreed between the customer and supplier, thereby reducing disputes.

Example

An organization is purchasing containers. The critical part of the container is the inside diameter of the curved corner. A specification has been drawn up for the radius of the corner and an AQL of 2.5 per cent outside specification agreed with the supplier.

Table 1 *AQL sampling information*

Inspection level	Code letter	Sample size	Acceptance criteria	
			Accept	Reject
I	G	32	2	3
II	J	80	5	6
III	K	125	7	8

Table 2 *Operating characteristic curves of sampling plans G, J and K*

Circumstances	G	J	K
Quality of submitted batch better than AQL	5% chance of rejection	2.5% chance of rejection	0.5% chance of rejection
Quality as bad as 5% defective	80% chance of acceptance	78% chance of acceptance	70% chance of acceptance
Quality as bad as 10% defective	37% chance of acceptance	19% chance of acceptance	7% chance of acceptance

The customer will be inspecting containers, so that defective units are to be inspected: the container is either right or wrong. The normal inspection level has been selected, the batch size is 1,000 containers and the batch is part of a series. Reference to BS6001 gives the information in Table 1.

The implications in terms of sampling risk of selecting one or other of these levels can be found by a study of the operating characteristic curves of plans G, J and K (Table 2).

It must be remembered that a lower inspection level does not imply a lower level of acceptable quality but an increase in the risks associated with the acceptance of a single batch. In a series of samples, we have to take into account the fact that some whole batches will be inspected and rejected 100 per cent and this will affect the outgoing quality. This allows you to make an informed judgement about which sampling plan is best for your use.

Reference

Guide to the Use of BS 6001: Sampling Procedures.

Method 2   Affinity diagram

Purpose

To organize large amounts of data in groups according to some form of natural affinity.

When to use

When a team is trying to ascertain customer needs with the intention of translating them into design requirements.

How to use

Each team member starts by writing ideas about customer needs on separate file cards. Then, laying the cards on a table without conversation to influence them, the team members should arrange them into the natural groups they can identify. Ideas which have an affinity for each other should be grouped together. An example of an affinity diagram is shown in Figure 1.

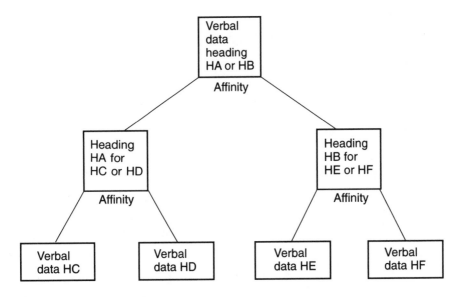

Figure 1   *Affinity diagram*

Benefits

Organizing data in the form of natural affinity can illustrate the associations rather than the strictly logical connections between customer needs.

Example

1 Define the subject that is to be considered, e.g. customer requirements for the product.
2 Arrange the data generated by the team under subordinate headings (see Figure 1):

   • Working in silence, arrange two cards which are related in some way.
   • Repeat this step.
   • Different opinions about the relationship between different data will be discovered.
   • Complete the work when all data have been organized according to a limited number of groups and different opinions have been resolved.
   • Find a heading for each data group.

Reference

B. Bergman and B. Klefsjo (1994) *Quality: from Customer Needs to Customer Satisfaction.* New York: McGraw-Hill.

Method 3   Arrow diagram

Purpose

To show the time required for solving a problem and which items can be done in parallel.

When to use

For day-to-day project and production planning and to ensure the most suitable time-scale for certain tasks.

How to use

The arrow diagram is a simplified critical path method of planning to show the optimum schedule for fulfilling a project and tracking its progress.

Benefits

To ensure the most suitable time planning for certain tasks.

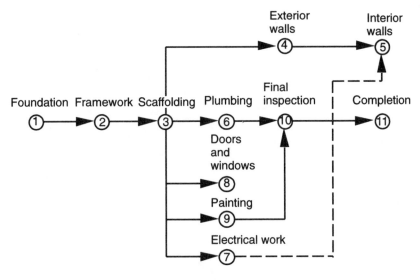

▶ Amount of time for each operation

–▶ Relation of work without time for each operation

Figure 1   *Arrow diagram*

Example

Figure 1 shows an arrow diagram used to plan the construction of a house, identifying:

- amount of time for each operation
- relation of work without time for each operation
- each specific operation.

Method 4   Benchmarking

Purpose

To identify and fill gaps in performance by putting in place best practice, thereby establishing superior performance.

When to use

As part of a total quality process when taking an independent look at performance by comparing it with that of others.

How to use

There are three distinct types of benchmarking which can be used by an organization progressively to stimulate the improvement process.

1 *Internal benchmarking* This is the comparison between functions, departments or a similar organization as a means of improving performance. The usual aim is to optimize process performance by the removal of errors.
2 *Competitive benchmarking* This is a cross-comparison within one industry sector aimed at establishing best practice through the identification of gaps between your own and your competitors' performance. This can be done on product, functional, departmental or on a company-wide basis.
3 *Comparative benchmarking* This is the comparison across all business sectors aimed at establishing best practice in all areas of operation.

The route to benchmarking is as follows:

1 Define the business mission. The *mission statement* lays down the business that you are in and can be translated into roles, goals and objectives; for example: 'To be one of the world's premier suppliers of pharmaceutical products, distinctive and successful in what we do.'
2 Identify the critical success factors (CSFs) that must be achieved to fulfil the mission. Each CSF must be necessary and, together, must be sufficient to achieve the mission. The CSFs are the absolute minimum set of aims to accomplish this. Examples for a pharmaceutical company might be:

• technical excellence in new products
• excellent suppliers
• well-qualified staff

- sound regulation

3 Identify the key business processes to be undertaken to achieve the CSFs. Processes describe how the work that is done in the business actually gets done. The list should be both necessary and sufficient to achieve the CSFs. Examples might be:

- manage the regulator
- manage raw material supplies
- manage patent protection

4 Flowchart the processes, identifying any gaps, dead ends or duplications. All internal customers and suppliers must be identified.
5 Set standards for the processes, identifying the level of performance that must be met. These should be as concise, unambiguous and measurable as possible.
6 Decide how the process performance can be measured.
7 Plan how to identify how others perform the same process. A typical format for doing this uses the following headings:

- description or process step
- standard
- measure
- questions

Benefits

Benchmarking provides an introduction to the idea of measurement, helps to focus on the mission and to identify measures or targets for key business processes. Companies that have previously been shy of measurement find that, through the introduction of benchmarking, it comes naturally. Benchmarking helps organizations to move away from being introspective towards being externally focused and close to their markets.

Example

A supplier to the motor industry used benchmarking to identify its key business processes. It then divided these into a number of sub-processes and set up improvement teams to flowchart and set standards and measures for the processes. One process identified was 'Introducing new products'. This broke down into nine sub-processes as follows:

- developing a customer requirement
- estimating costs
- authorizing new products
- identifying suppliers
- developing new tooling

- purchasing new supplies
- developing a bill of materials
- writing new specifications
- developing a new production plan

The team drew outline flowcharts for each of the sub-processes and then began to draw detailed flowcharts. It quickly became apparent that all product designs were being treated equally, whether important to the company or not. The consequence was that minor designs were being forced through the total process and were making it difficult for major designs to progress. The amount of variability in the process made it very difficult to estimate times and keep to schedules.

The organization agreed on two separate processes, depending upon the importance of the design, and set standards on process steps in terms of both time and completeness. Having formalized their own processes, they then began to compare them with others outside the organization.

References

R.C. Camp (1989) *Benchmarking: the Search for Industry Best Practices that Lead to Superior Performance*. Milwaukee: ASQC Press.

B. Karlof and S. Ostblom (1994) *Benchmarking: a Signpost to Excellence in Quality and Productivity*. New York: Wiley.

Method 5   Consensus reaching

Purpose

To give a team a methodical way of examining alternatives to reach a collective conclusion which all team members can accept.

When to use

When a team is examining different courses of action or choosing possible solutions to a problem.

How to use

There are six steps involved:

1 All team members think individually what the options are and each makes a list of his or her own ideas.
2 Participants are invited in turn to read out their suggestions. These are recorded on a flip chart. Participants are not allowed to discuss the ideas at this stage.
3 After everyone has listed their suggestions, group members are allowed to add to the list any new ideas as they think of them.
4 The group leader then checks that all suggestions are understood and seeks clarification if necessary.
5 The ideas are counted. Everyone individually assigns them points. If there are 12 ideas, start with 12 points for the most important.
6 Participants now reveal their own top choices which are recorded on a flip chart. The discussion then starts and the ideas that the majority choose are debated until consensus is reached.

If necessary, the procedure is repeated with a reduced number of ideas.

Benefits

People often cling to their own ideas and are reluctant to consider the suggestions of others when making a decision. The technique permits a decision to be made without taking a final vote that can leave some team members feeling isolated. The procedure allows a group to reach the best solution – not a compromise solution – and to harness all members' commitment to making the solution work. The technique works best in groups of 8–12 people.

Example

An organization was in a serious cash-flow crisis and the management team was seeking ways, first, to stop further damage and, secondly, reverse the situation. The problem was compounded by different professional and personal interests within the group. Consensus reaching was used as a means of getting the group's agreement to a series of measures which were unpalatable but necessary.

Method 6   Contingency planning

Purpose

To avoid 'firefighting' and waste of resources by planning for contingencies in the completion of a project.

When to use

When planning to implement a project.

How to use

There are six key steps involved:

1   List, in a logical sequence, the steps to be taken to achieve successful completion of the project.
2   Examine each step and decide which are the most critical areas and where it is most likely that a problem will occur. These are, for example, where deadlines are tight, where other departments are involved or where approval is needed.
3   Use brainstorming to discover the likely cause of these problems. Remember that you are looking at the serious problems, not all problems.
4   When you have identified the potential likely causes, list them clearly.
5   Decide where preventive action can be taken: how can the problem be removed or minimized?
6   Modify the original plan to take the preventive action into account.

Benefits

By taking into account possible problems before they arise, the implementation of plans can be made smoother and more certain.

Example

An organization is planning to register a training course before a set deadline and is drawing up a contingency plan. In order to be successful with the project, the project manager examined the most critical areas where problems might occur, i.e. tight deadlines, involvement of other departments where appraisals are needed etc. He then modified his plan for successful registration of the training course.

Method 7   Cost-benefit analysis

Purpose

To estimate the real cost and benefits of a project under consideration.

When to use

A problem-solving team would use cost-benefit analysis to find out if a solution is practical in terms of cost.

How to use

This simple technique involves evaluating all the costs associated with implementing a particular project, and comparing them with the expected benefit. The evaluation usually covers a three- or five-year period.

The technique can also be used without actual cost figures, but using weightings. This is particularly applicable when dealing with organizational or 'human' problems.

Benefits

Some solutions to problems are relatively easy to evaluate, but often a case has to be made for implementing a particular solution. Cost-benefit analysis enables a team to make a case for a solution being adopted.

Example

A problem-solving group had discovered that key punch error was the first major cause of incorrect data entry. They identified various ways of putting this right, including the purchase of a new piece of hardware costing £5,000. The cost-benefit analysis looked like this:

Costs year 1	£
Machine	5,000
Re-wiring and installation	1,500
Cost of re-training	1,200
Lost time cost	1,000
Total cost	8,700

Benefits year 1	£
Re-work reduced by 20%	3,750
Reduced reconciliation costs	2,500
Total cost	6,250

Benefits year 2	£
Re-work reduced by 20%	3,750
Reduced reconciliation costs	2,500
Total cost	6,250

Comparing the costs and benefits over two years shows:

	Costs £	*Benefits* £	*Profit* £
Year 1	8,700	6,250	−2,450
Year 2	0	6,250	6,250
Total	8,700	12,500	3,800

In two years the new equipment will re-pay the cost of purchase and generate additional savings.

Method 8 Criteria testing

Purpose

To evaluate and compare alternative solutions to a problem by rating them against a list of criteria.

When to use

When you need to decide which ideas to choose from a shortlist. The technique allows ideas or solutions to be ranked so that comparisons can be made.

How to use

There are five steps involved.

1 State the criteria requirements of a good solution.
2 List the criteria in order of importance, then place them across the top of a flip chart.
3 List the alternative solutions or ideas down the left-hand side of the flip chart. When this is complete, form a matrix.
4 For each option in turn, estimate how well it meets each criterion. A scale of 1–10 can be used: 1 relates to the best, lowest cost, fastest solution etc. If a group of people is involved, ask each person to estimate individually and take the average score of the group.
5 For each option, add together the scores. The preferred solution is the one with the lowest total score.

If, during step 4, the scores are very different, stop and check that everyone in the group has the same understanding of the criteria. It might emerge that someone has a hidden agenda and is rating accordingly. Alternatively, new information might arise at this stage.

An alternative to using a 10-point scale is to rank the options on each criterion, the best choice scoring 1 etc. The selected option is again the one with the lowest total score.

Benefits

Simply voting on ideas or forcing a weighting system can be very divisive. Criteria testing allows a group to make a decision with a common set of

Criteria / Options	Cost 1 = Low 10 = High	Time 1 = Fast 10 = Slow	Union 1 = Easy 10 = Hard	Approval 1 = Hard 10 = Easy	Total
Buy additional	10	10	1	10	31
Contract out	5	1	5	5	16
Change working practice	1	5	5	1	12
Do nothing	8	1	1	8	18

Figure 1   *Criteria testing*

assumptions. Done this way, the commitment to the solution will be greater.

Example

A company had a problem with low utilization of desktop publishing equipment and examined alternative ways of increasing throughput. Figure 1 shows a completed criteria testing matrix for the four identified options. The option selected was to change working practice to allow those carrying out the task more say in the scheduling of work.

Method 9   Customers' contingency table

Purpose

To understand the needs of both internal and external customers for the fulfilment of customer satisfaction.

When to use

When a team is trying to learn the level of customer satisfaction of both internal and external customers. Failure to satisfy the customer may put the company out of business.

How to use

List both your internal and external customers and their needs, i.e. what they require; what they expect; and what would exceed their expectations. This can be generated with the help of brainstorming, mind mapping or a combination of both.

LEVEL OF CUSTOMERS' NEEDS

	Must	Expectation	Above expectation
External	Receive product order	Easy to order Added value Helpful service	24-hour delivery Free shipping
Internal	Receive correct information	Easy to deal with the process To be treated like a valuable customer	Full cooperation

CUSTOMERS

Figure 1   *Customers' contingency table*

Benefits

It helps you to understand the association between your customers and their level of requirements.

Example

A customers' contingency table is shown in Figure 1. Here, *must* is the *minimum* customer requirement. Failing in this will cause dissatisfaction.

Method 10 Deming wheel (PDCA)

Purpose

A management concept suggested by Deming to satisfy the quality requirements of the customer by using the cycle: plan, do, check and action.

When to use

For the development of a new product based on the requirements of the customer.

How to use

Develop teamwork between the company's various functions, i.e. product development, manufacturing, sales and market research. Use the plan (P), do (D), check (C) and action (A) cycle as shown in Figure 1. Discuss details of each stage of the cycle. The cycle, or wheel, must be constantly rotating.

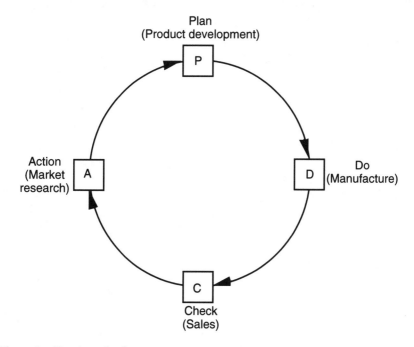

Figure 1   *Deming wheel*

1 *Plan*: When a problem is detected in product development, first find the causes of the problem. The decision to make changes must be based on facts, and therefore it is necessary to obtain the data to detect the causes of error and variation.
2 *Do*: When the cause of a problem is detected, a quality improvement team will take responsibility for carrying through the necessary steps to solve the problem.
3 *Check*: When proper steps have been taken to solve the problem, an investigation will take place to check whether the improvement process was successful.
4 *Action*: If the steps taken were successful, the new and better quality level should be accepted. If the steps taken were not successful, then the PDCA cycle should be repeated.

Benefits

It will help to ensure that the customer is always fully satisfied.

Example

A company implementing the TQM process used the Deming wheel for achieving continuous improvement of the various business processes in order to develop quality improvement of the whole organization.

Reference

W.E. Deming (1986) *Out of the Crisis*. Cambridge, Massachusetts: MIT Press.

Method 11   Departmental purpose analysis (DPA)

Purpose

To review the internal customer–supplier relationship.

When to use

When you want to understand the nature and cost of quality in the department, i.e. to improve interdepartmental quality.

How to use

Ask pertinent questions about the department such as:

1   What is the role of the department?
2   Does my boss agree?
3   Why is this department doing this activity?
4   Is it being done the way the 'customer' department would want it?
5   What impact does the activity have on the prime objective of satisfying the requirements of the external customer?

Benefits

By establishing the above information, both within departments and across departmental barriers, DPA helps managers address improvements in interdepartmental quality for the benefit of the organization.

Examples

Examples of key tasks and activities involved in DPA are as follows:

Key tasks

- coordinate total quality
- manage company quality system
- implement vendor assessment system
- maintain customer returns system
- maintain scrap reporting system
- maintain finished product audit system
- maintain quarantine store

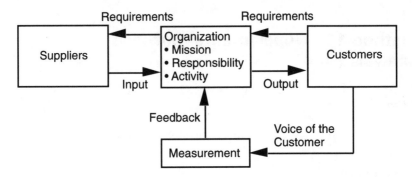

Figure 1   *Departmental purpose analysis*

Activities

- update project plan
- organize Board steering group
- manage consultant interface
- identify training (quality) needs
- agree measures
- agree progress reporting system
- organize trainer training

Departmental purpose analysis focuses on the customer. When the requirements of the customer are seen as the responsibility of the department an effective measurement system can be adopted (as given in Figure 1).

Reference

D. Bell, P. McBride and G. Wilson (1994) *Managing Quality*. London: Butterworth/ Heinemann.

Method 12   Error proofing (pokayoke)

Purpose

To design an operation in such a way that specific errors are prevented from causing major problems to the customer.

When to use

It can be used when defects occur and require 100 per cent inspection, immediate feedback and action at the:

- source of raw materials and components
- start of the production process
- production points where an error may occur

How to use

In a pokayoke system, carry out automatic continuous inspection and, if abnormalities occur, then provide feedback and take action. However, before processing can begin, one has to halt the process, obtain feedback and execute necessary action.

Benefits

Unlike statistical quality control systems, in which a fairly long time elapses between the 'check' stage and the execution of feedback and action, pokayoke minimizes defects by carrying out feedback and action immediately at a low cost.

Examples

A large steel press is automatically monitored for wear. If the thickness becomes less than a specified amount, an alarm sounds and action has to be taken to rectify the error.

A second example involves a car manufacturer which was concerned to prevent omission of car door pockets in production. The operation in which pockets were mounted on the door trim involved three specifications, and workers occasionally neglected to mount the pockets, or mounted them incorrectly, according to their attention to work in progress.

To improve the process, door trims were exposed to a detector which recognized whether pockets were missing. If right and left pockets had been reversed or if a pocket had not been mounted, a buzzer sounded, air stopped flowing to the screw-tightening lock and the operation could not proceed. In this way, instances of pocket omission were eliminated.

Method 13   Force analysis

Purpose

To identify external and internal forces at work when developing a contingency plan.

When to use

Use this method before developing a list of potential problems for your problem prevention plan.

How to use

1   Draw a circle.
2   Write down the external forces trying to keep the plan from occurring (outside the circle).

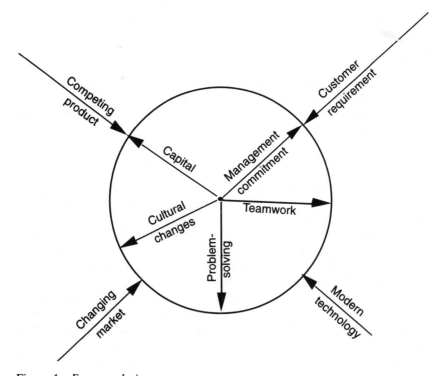

Figure 1   *Force analysis*

3 Write down the internal forces trying to accomplish the plan (inside the circle).

4 Denote the strength of the force by the length of an arrow.

Benefits

Powerful method for helping to develop a contingency plan by providing a graphic illustration of external and internal processes at work.

Example

External and internal forces for developing a business plan are shown in Figure 1. Here, force analysis helps to identify the forces which are helping you to accomplish your purpose and those which are resisting your efforts. In this situation, customer requirement can be met by management commitment. However, external forces, such as modern technology, and internal forces, such as cultural change, might resist the development of the business plan.

Method 14   Gannt charts

Purpose

For planning the steps necessary to implement quality improvement.

When to use

When a team has decided upon a project and is planning its implementation, Gannt charts are useful for scheduling the events necessary to complete the improvement activity.

How to use

Gannt charts are very easy to use:

1 Break down the implementation plan into achievable tasks and activities.
2 Estimate how long each task will take and then set a realistic completion date.
3 Break down the steps into a logical sequence. Lines denote when a task is due to commence and end. The relationship over time between each task is immediately visible.
4 Assess each step individually, identifying:

- any issue that stops you completing a stated task (this is noted as a key issue)
- any dependent task that must be completed before another task is begun.

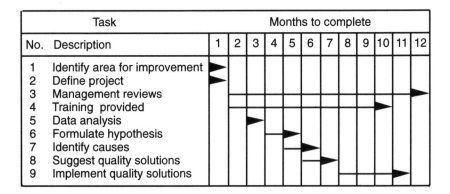

Task		Months to complete											
No.	Description	1	2	3	4	5	6	7	8	9	10	11	12
1	Identify area for improvement												
2	Define project												
3	Management reviews												
4	Training provided												
5	Data analysis												
6	Formulate hypothesis												
7	Identify causes												
8	Suggest quality solutions												
9	Implement quality solutions												

Figure 1   *Gannt chart for the implementation of a quality improvement project*

Benefits

The visual representation of tasks helps identify the key issues and brings into the open the steps needed for successful completion. It also makes it easy to see when deadlines slip and changes to the plan have to be made.

Example

In the example shown in Figure 1, an organization is using a Gannt chart to plan the implementation of a quality improvement project. The time-scale is given in months. It can be seen that tasks 3 and 4 cannot be deferred without delay to the total plan. Task 5 is a key issue in that, without data analysis, the quality improvement process cannot be implemented.

Method 15   ISO 9000

Purpose

To demonstrate to yourself, your customers and an independent assessment body that you have an effective quality management system in place.

When to use

When trying to formalize operations to ensure consistency of approach.

How to use

There are 13 steps associated with building a quality management system (QMS).

1 Obtain management understanding of, and commitment to, the quality management approach.
2 Define the scope of the activities to be included in the QMS.
3 Define the organizational structure and responsibilities of those within the scope of the QMS.
4 Audit the existing systems and procedures against the requirements of the standard.
5 Develop a plan to write the necessary procedures.
6 Train sufficient personnel to write their own procedures.
7 Draft and edit the procedures and gain agreement to them.
8 Compile a draft quality manual.
9 Implement the system on a trial basis.
10 Train internal auditors to carry out audits of the system and its operation.
11 Revise the operation of the system in light of the results of audits and other information.
12 Apply for registration (sometimes called third-party approval) from an accredited body.
13 Maintain the system by internal audit, using it as an opportunity to improve.

Benefit

By establishing a consistent approach, it becomes easier to ensure that tasks are carried out in the same way whoever does them. This in turn ensures consistent quality for customers.

Example

A QMS normally contains four levels of documentation. These are:

1   A *quality policy manual*: this is a policy document, a statement of intent about *what* you intend to do.
2   A *quality procedures manual*: this is a more detailed series of documents detailing *how* you will carry out the 'whats' of the quality policy manual.
3   *Quality records*: these are the proofs that the 'hows' have been carried out.
4   *Work instructions*: these are the small details that explain how specific tasks are carried out. Each procedure may have several work instructions for different products or services.

References

BS EN ISO 9000–1: *Selection and Use.*
BS EN ISO 9001: *QA Design.*

Method 16   Just in time (JIT)

Purpose

To deliver the raw materials or components to the production line to arrive just in time when they are needed.

When to use

When you want to minimize or eliminate stocks in order to prevent the organization from incurring unproductive cost.

How to use

The production process uses the 'pull system', whereby the material is not received from the supplier or requested from the preceding production phase until it is needed to sustain production.

Benefits

It helps to eliminate stocks in order to prevent unproductive stock cost. The benefit to four companies of using JIT can be seen in Table 1.

Example

JIT was developed by Toyota Motor Company. In 1984 Toyota agreed to re-open General Motors' old plant in California as a joint venture. A new stamping plant was built next to GM's old plant, so that various stamping could be produced in small batches when needed. These components had previously been made at other GM factories, which meant that car assembly was dependent on large amounts of components being sent by train from other factories. The adoption of Toyota's production system (JIT) in GM's factory also meant that these two systems were inseparable, and productivity and quality at this old factory were acceptable.

Table 1 *Benefits of JIT*

Company	Reduced inventory (%)	Reduced lead times (%)	Reduced re-work (%)	Reduced space (%)
A	94	95	50	40
B	82	95	51	70
C	75	92	372	58
D	94	70	75	40

Method 17   Kaizen

Purpose

A Japanese term meaning 'change for the better', the concept implies a continuous improvement in all company functions at all levels.

When to use

The term is so common in Japan that it is used in all aspects of life.

How to use

The *kaizen* concept is based on people's commitment and participation by using their knowledge and experience, and can therefore be established through quality circles and suggestion schemes. It can be used in both manufacturing and business activities.

Benefits

Given the same basic technology, *kaizen* can help to lead to a higher productivity rate and high-quality products.

Example

Dahlgaard et al. (1990) surveyed companies in Japan, Korea and Denmark, and found that the number of companies with quality circles was about 97 per cent in Japan and Korea, but only 12 per cent in Denmark. About 70–80 per cent of employees in Japan and Korea took part in quality circles, but only 12 per cent in Denmark.

Suggestion schemes, with or without a reward system, can be found in more than 95 per cent of companies in Japan and Korea. The corresponding figure for Denmark is only 40–50 per cent.

In Japan, *kaizen* activities are in addition to maintenance of the process and they can therefore improve the quality of service and products with limited investment.

References

J.J. Dahlgaard, G.K. Kanji, K. Kristensen (1990) 'A comparative study of quality control methods and principles in Japan, Korea and Denmark', *Total Quality Management*, 1: 115–32.
M. Imai (1986) *Kaizen: The Key to Japan's Competitive Success*. New York: Random House.

Method 18   Mystery shopping

Purpose

A technique involving looking at your business from the outside and measuring the efficiency of your own key processes from the customer's viewpoint.

When to use

When measuring customer satisfaction. Mystery shopping is often used during benchmarking exercises or as part of a motivation programme.

How to use

An organization first develops an understanding of its own key processes and behaviours and then deliberately makes a comparison with the competition. Alternatively, a company can compare the performance of its own staff.

Benefits

Many 'employee of the month' schemes are based on 'it must be Dave's turn', rather than on any objective measure. Mystery shopping bestows an understood measure and gives credibility to such schemes. Used externally, mystery shopping gives a first-hand measure to compare competitors with your own performance.

Examples

An advertising company decides that one of its key processes is taking a brief from a client. The company develops a set of measures that it wishes to use. These measures could be:

- speed of initial response
- understanding of brief
- speed of reply to brief
- quality of response

The mystery shopping is then done in several simple steps:

1 The company, using an outside agent, builds up a typical brief from a client.
2 The company decides which competitors to include in the study.
3 The outside agent approaches both the company and the competitors and, presenting it as though it were a real brief, asks for the same response from each.
4 Each company is rated against all the measures.
5 The results are reported and an action plan agreed.

A second example concerns a motor trade distributor who wishes to compare the performance of its own sales force across all its outlets as part of a motivation programme. The company first develops a set of successful selling behaviours that it expects its sales team to exhibit. These could be:

• welcome on entering the showroom
• understanding customer needs
• sending information as requested
• follow-up telephone call

The company, using an outside agent, visits each of its own showrooms, posing as a real customer. The sales team are rated against the agreed criteria and the results used to plan training and to recognize desired behaviour.

Reference

Sarah Cook (1992) *Customer Care*. New York: Kogan Page.

Method 19   Objective ranking

Purpose

Helps to place your current activity in perspective and enable you to understand the purpose of your efforts.

When to use

When you want to know where to start.

How to use

1   Collect a list of potential objectives.
2   Write down each objective on a card.
3   Eliminate any objective which is not appropriate.

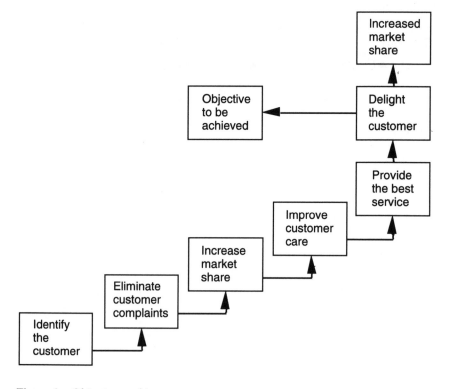

Figure 1   *Objective ranking*

4 Rank objective list according to highest or lowest purpose.
5 Check the list with customer needs.
6 Find the minimum action that could be used to satisfy customer requirements.
7 Pick the optimum objective which can be achieved with the available resources.
8 Pick up the objective from the list that meets customer requirements and can be achieved by the group.

Benefits

It gives a wider understanding of various activities when transforming each step into a process of productive change.

Example

Suppose that the objective to be accomplished is to delight the customer. Objective ranking should connect one objective to another, supporting the next higher one, as shown in Figure 1.

Method 20   Pareto analysis

Purpose

To separate the most important causes of a problem from the many trivial. Also, to identify the most important problems for a team to work on. Pareto analysis was first used by Wilfredo Pareto, an Italian economist.

When to use

When a team is analysing data relating to a problem to decide which are the most important factors to be tackled first to have the most impact on the problem.

Table 1 *Pareto analysis*

Error description	Error code	Count	% of total	Cumul. %
Wrong component	33	3,138	22.95	22.95
Missing component	51	2,541	18.59	41.54
Not soldered	71	1,382	10.11	51.65
Other solder/PB problems	92	1,307	9.56	61.21
Wrongly inserted	54	1,142	8.35	69.56
Shorts-solder side	77	831	6.08	75.64
Electrical defect	12	722	5.28	80.92
Wrong placement	53	687	5.03	85.95
Shorts caused by components	56	649	4.75	90.70
Test equipment . . .	94	523	3.83	94.52
Not correctly inserted	61	237	1.73	96.25
PB faults	91	178	1.30	97.56
Electrical out of tolerance	15	83	0.61	98.16
Mechanical defect	11	78	0.57	98.73
SMD alignment	58	59	0.43	99.17
Shorts-component side	78	51	0.37	99.54
Protrusion length	46	23	0.17	99.71
Documents progr. faults	93	19	0.14	99.85
Additional component	52	8	0.06	99.90
SMD tombstone-effect	59	6	0.04	99.95
Missing label	95	3	0.02	99.97
Dirt	22	1	0.01	99.98
Broken solder joint	76	1	0.01	99.99
Ball-shaped solder joint	82	0	0.00	99.99
Component damaged	41	1	0.01	100.00
Total		13 671	100.00	

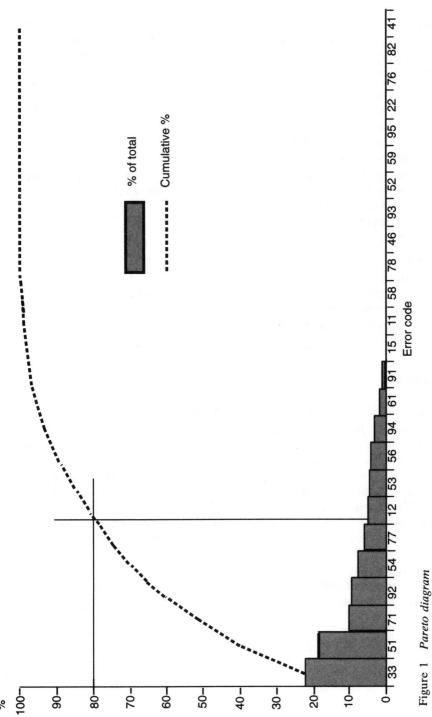

Figure 1 *Pareto diagram*

How to use

Pareto analysis is sometimes called the 80/20 rule. This means that 80 per cent of the problems are caused by 20 per cent of the activities and it is this important 20 per cent that should be concentrated on. There are six simple steps involved:

1 List the activities or causes in a table and count the number of times each occurs.
2 Place these in descending order of magnitude in the table.
3 Calculate the total for the whole list.
4 Calculate the percentage of the total that each cause represents.
5 Draw a Pareto diagram with the vertical axis showing the percentage and the horizontal axis the activity or cause. The cumulative curve can be drawn to show the cumulative percentage from all causes.
6 Interpret the results.

Benefits

When working in teams it can be difficult to reach agreement when people with different opinions want to follow different courses of action. Pareto analysis brings the facts to the attention of all members of the team to aid decision-making.

Example

Following manufacture of a printed circuit board, the board is tested to identify any faults. Table 1 shows the error description, error code and count of the number of errors. The percentage of the total and the cumulative percentage is also given.

Figure 1 gives the error code on the horizontal axis and the percentage on the vertical axis. The cumulative percentage curve is shown as a dotted line. The Pareto diagram shows clearly that six out of 25 error types (24 per cent) account for nearly 80 per cent of the total number of errors. The errors that must be reduced to have a major impact on the overall situation are clearly shown.

It would also be possible to draw a Pareto diagram showing the cost of errors or the importance of different errors, if these factors were more important than simple occurrence alone.

Reference

P. Spenley (1992) *World Class Performance through Total Quality*. London: Chapman and Hall.

Method 21   Potential problem analysis (PPA)

Purpose

To examine plans to identify what can go wrong with them, so that preventive action can be taken.

When to use

Potential problem analysis (PPA) is used when plans are first drawn up and subsequently at planning reviews to anticipate future problems and plan contingency actions.

How to use

PPA is a very simple technique for a team to examine plans. There are eight steps:

1 Draw up the plan in time order.
2 Flowchart the plan, identifying all the key steps where specific outputs are needed.
3 At each key step brainstorm the problems that could occur.
4 Rate the potential problems using the following scheme:

   • *Likelihood*   10 (very likely) to 1 (very unlikely)
   • *Severity*   10 (catastrophic) to 1 (mild)

   Multiply the likelihood by the severity to get the potential problem risk (PPR) number.
5 For each potential problem, identify the likely causes. This is done first for problems with a high PPR number. All problems with a PPR above 50 or a likelihood or severity above 7 must be prevented.
6 For each cause, brainstorm the courses of action that could be taken to prevent it happening.
7 For problems that can be prevented, take the necessary steps to remove the potential cause.
8 For problems that cannot be prevented, draw up contingency plans to rectify the problem if it occurs.

Benefits

By anticipating problems with plans before they occur, and either removing them by prevention or drawing up contingency plans, smooth implementation of projects can be achieved.

Example

An organization was planning to hold its AGM in a Central London location and used PPA to assist with the planning of the event to ensure that no problems occurred.

Method 22   Problem prevention plan

Purpose

To anticipate what can go wrong and plan to prevent problems.

When to use

When you need to analyse potential problems and their causes.

How to use

1 For each specific task write down a list of potential problems.
2 For each problem, rate the chances of it happening and the seriousness if it did happen.
3 For most serious problems, write down the potential causes and chance of occurrence.
4 For most likely causes, decide what prevention strategies can be put in place.
5 Integrate prevention strategies into your plan.

Benefits

It helps prevent potential problems from actually taking place.

Potential problem	Chances High Medium Low			Seriousness High Medium Low		
Person in charge ill	X					X
Computer out of order		X		X		
Badly produced document	X			X		
Program bug		X			X	

Figure 1   *Problem prevention plan*

Example

Potential problems in delivery and order documentation are rated in Figure 1. Here, the likelihood of a serious problem lies in a badly produced document. Toner could be a cause of this problem. Hence, a regular check of the toner will be part of the problem prevention plan.

Method 23 Process decision programme chart

Purpose

To focus on possible sequences to help lead to a desirable result and contingency planning.

When to use

When designing a new plan to achieve a desired result, and to avoid certain undesired outcomes.

How to use

A process decision programme chart can be used to design a plan to achieve your desired objective, to deal with problems encountered while implementing the plan and to make correct decisions to enhance the plan, thereby achieving the objective. In addition, the chart can be used to conceive counter-measures to avoid an undesirable situation by simulating a process of events leading to an undesirable result.

Benefits

It helps to plan to obtain a desirable outcome.

Example

The process decision programme chart given in Figure 1 shows the process which can help to secure a contract.

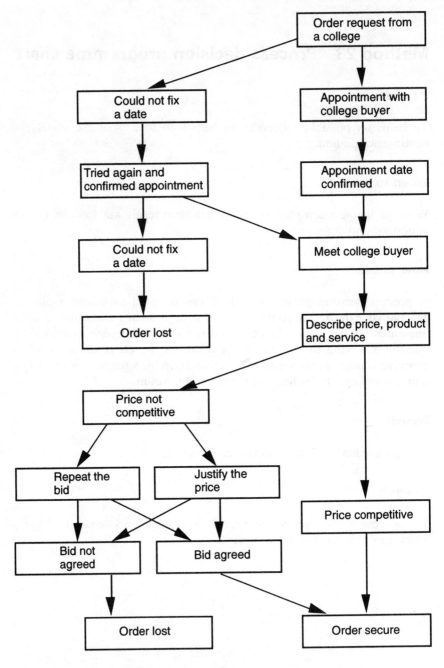

Figure 1   *Process decision programme chart*

Method 24 Programme evaluation and review (PER) technique

Purpose

To establish a planning technique for complex and multi-level projects.

When to use

When you need to meet a deadline to complete a complex task.

How to use

1 Describe the task to be completed.
2 Establish the previous task to be performed in order to complete the present task.
3 Work backwards from the completion date (see Figure 1), indicating the task within a circle.
4 Present the task which preceded it in circles and indicate the required completion date.
5 Draw an arrow from the previous task to the present task.

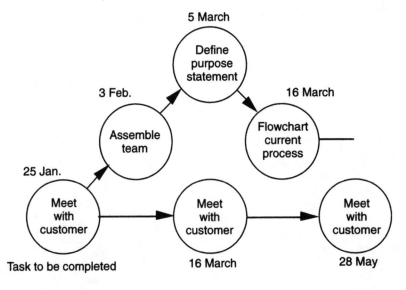

Figure 1 *PER technique*

6 Continue until all the tasks have been taken into account.
7 Review the diagram and establish the critical path which requires the most amount of time to complete the project.

See also *Critical path analysis* (Method 33).

Benefits

It helps to match delivery and order documentation to complete the schedule for a project.

Example

Figure 1 matches delivery and other documentation by PER process.

Reference

D.R. Anderson, D.J. Sweeney and T.A. Williams (1994) *An Introduction to Management Sciences*. New York: West.

Method 25 Quality circles

Purpose

A special type of small group activity which forms a vehicle for the development of individuals.

When to use

Quality circles are especially useful in the later stages of a total quality process when individuals in their own work areas begin to tackle their own problems. They lead to self-regulation in work groups.

How to use

Quality circles are small groups of between three and 12 people who do the same or similar work, voluntarily meeting together regularly for about an hour per week in paid time. Usually under the leadership of their own supervisor or manager, they are trained to identify, analyse and solve some of the problems in their own work, wherever possible implementing the solutions themselves.

Circle leaders and members should be trained in the following techniques:

- brainstorming
- tally charts
- concentration diagrams
- Pareto analysis
- histograms
- cause and effect analysis
- control charts

Quality circles are very different from action teams and task forces, which are initiated by management to solve a specific problem and are disbanded when that problem has been solved. Quality circles are formed and trained; they then identify their own problems. When those problems have been solved, the circle remains in place and identifies further problems to solve.

Benefits

Quality circles give structure and focus to improvement and allow it to occur in a planned way, whereas simply asking for suggestions could generate too many problems with no means to handle them.

There are dangers in using quality circles too early in the process: they may be seen as another management fad or as managers seeking to abrogate responsibility.

Example

A company in the Potteries set up quality circles to allow all employees to contribute their own ideas to the benefit of the whole company. In the first year more than 25 circle presentations were made and successfully implemented.

Reference

David Hutchins (1985) *Quality Circles Handbook*. London: Pitman.

Method 26 Quality function deployment (QFD)

Purpose

A technique or discipline for optimizing the process of developing and producing new products on the basis of customer need.

When to use

During design, commissioning or post-commissioning to translate customer requirements into company requirements. The technique can be used in research, product development, engineering, manufacturing, marketing and distribution areas.

How to use

QFD is a five-stage process that takes a design from customer requirements into a plan and schedule (see Bossert, 1991; Day, 1993).

1 The first stage is identifying customer needs or wants. These are usually characteristics directly attributable to the product or service, such as what it looks like, how it feels, how long it lasts, how it compares with the competition. At this stage the requirements are not usually measurable.
2 These requirements are then translated into technical specifications through the use of technical experts. At this stage the requirements become measurable.
3 The technical specifications are then turned into end-product specifications. These are called 'critical part characteristics'. Taken together, they are both necessary and sufficient to lead to an end product meeting the customer specification.
4 The fourth stage is to design the process to deliver the product or service. In other words, decide how to turn the design into reality.
5 The final stage is to plan the activities necessary to produce the required output.

Figure 1 illustrates a typical QFD matrix, often called the 'House of Quality'. The left side of the matrix comprises customer requirements as described in (1) above. The top of the matrix shows the organization's requirements as described in (2). The right side of the matrix gives the planning considerations to produce the output. The roof of the house

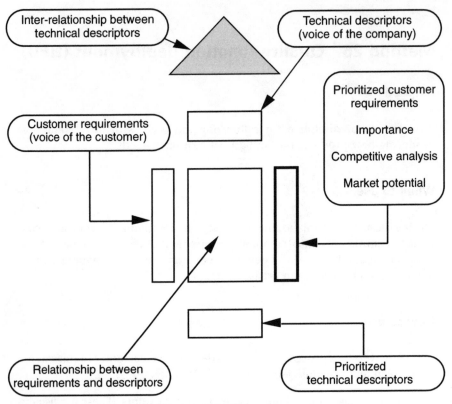

Figure 1   *QFD matrix: the House of Quality*

shows the fourth stage where decisions are made to turn the design into reality.

The central part of the matrix comprises the relationship between customer needs and design requirements. This is where the requirements become a specification.

It is usual to use the following schema to show relationships in the matrix:

◎   Some relationship
◉   Strong relationship
△   Weak relationship
☐   No relationship

Benefits

Quality function deployment encourages organizations to focus on the process itself rather than just on the product or service. By establishing correlations between what is wanted and how it is to be delivered, the vital aspects become more visible, aiding decision-making.

Example

The model shown in Figure 1 gives only the basic elements of QFD. The House of Quality aids the process of idea generation to develop new products on the basis of customer need.

Method 27   Relation diagram

Purpose

To illustrate the relationship between problems and ideas in complex situations. Also to identify meaningful categories from a mass of ideas when relationships are difficult to determine.

When to use

When a topic is so complicated that relations between different ideas cannot be established through conventional reasoning and the problem in question is exclusively a symptom of a more fundamental underlying problem.

How to use

The development of the relation diagram should be conducted in teams. The team writes each idea in a circle and clusters the circles in proximity to each other. It then identifies which idea strongly influences another and uses arrows to indicate the direction of influence. The results are evaluated by identifying ideas that have the most arrows entering or exiting.

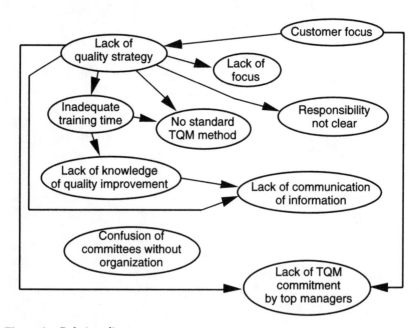

Figure 1   *Relation diagram*

Benefits

It identifies relationship between problems and ideas in complex situations.

Example

Figure 1 presents the results of a team brainstorming session which identified ten major issues involved in developing an organization's quality plan.

Method 28   Teamwork

Purpose

To organize activity which requires a number of people to collaborate and work together for a common goal.

When to use

When people with different but complementary responsibilities, knowledge or abilities can contribute to the development of a strategy or solution to a problem important to the company.

How to use

Teamwork requires the cooperative effort and contribution of a number of people with a common goal or objective.

Benefits

It helps to develop a quality strategy or to achieve solutions to a problem vital to the company.

Example

Quality improvement teams, universally adopted by every company engaged in quality improvement, are an example of teamwork. *Quality circles* (Method 25) are another way of using the benefits of teamwork.

Teamwork can provide a focus for a group of people in a task force looking at cross-functional problems. One organization which had previously had an autocratic style of management, where managers told everyone what to do and then disciplined them when they did not follow instructions, always experienced difficulty in introducing change. There was an atmosphere of suspicion, and most significant change had to be negotiated through the powerful trade union.

By making significant change part of a TQM process and moving towards cross-departmental teams to define and solve problems, the organization was able to use the power of the team to suggest change and then to implement changes at a pace that would previously have been impossible.

Method 29 Total productive maintenance

Purpose

To help a process which aims at making the most effective and efficient use of existing production structures.

When to use

When an organization needs to improve its maintenance system and to educate operators in maintenance techniques.

How to use

Use all the company's functions and personnel to contribute to maintenance through both individual effort and teamwork.

Benefits

It provides effective and efficient use of existing production methods. It establishes a thorough system of preventive maintenance, condition monitoring etc. for the equipment's entire lifespan.

Example

A typical procedure for total production maintenance is as follows:

1 Develop and agree the maintenance strategy and identify priorities for the key items of plant and equipment in terms of their contribution to operating plans. Take account of the company's manufacturing philosophy and its manufacturing organization.
2 Establish target levels of maintenance dependent on plant and equipment availability and identify those items which demand close attention and control.
3 Review the maintenance organization, especially in its relationship with production planning and scheduling and production itself, addressing, for example, the advantages of, and barriers to, combining responsibilities for maintenance, particularly where production staff can contribute to the provision of information on operating difficulties or diagnostic routines.

4   Investigate the application of relevant technology, e.g. condition monitoring, and its possible future integration with any existing statistical process control.

5   Establish a framework for a maintenance planning and information system and its interface with, for example, the company's production planning and control systems.

6   Determine the relevance, scope and specification of a computer-based planned maintenance system.

7   Specify the reference points (i.e. current situation), appropriate ratios, yardsticks and reporting system to measure maintenance *value for money*, building upon any current controls already implemented.

8   Identify training requirements of both operators and the maintenance department.

9   Estimate the bottom line gain the company can expect as a result of any improvement programme.

10 Specify the spares support function (i.e. provisioning, stocking, procurement systems and procedures).

11 Pull all of the above together as a 'maintenance improvement plan' which clearly identifies the objectives, activities, time-scale and resources required to implement and achieve standards of good practice.

Reference

Seiichi Nakamima (1988) *Introduction to TPM*. Cambridge, Massachusetts: Productivity Press.

Method 30 Why–how charting

Purpose

When thinking in both abstract and concrete terms, and needing to move between the two, why–how charting enables a goal to be translated into action.

When to use

Either individually or as part of a group, the method can be used to:
- map the implications of a goal
- generate alternative statements of a problem
- develop alternative solutions
- present findings and stimulate discussion
- begin the planning process

How to use

There are three simple stages:
1 Write the goal or problem in the centre of a flip chart.
2 Ask a series of 'why' questions and plot the answers on the page above the goal.
3 Ask a series of 'how' questions and plot the answers on the page below the goal.

Benefits

By bridging between strategic and tactical thinking, the technique makes it possible to challenge goals, perhaps revealing new ways of meeting them, while simultaneously planning to meet them.

Example

In the example below the problem is that the managing director is overloaded. The desired goal is to reduce the loading.

Why? To generate new business
Why? To devote more time to marketing
Goal Reduce the MD's loading
How? Identify what can be delegated
How? Discuss with staff their roles

Method 31   Zero defects

Purpose

To allow teams to experience the success involved in meeting ever more demanding targets without demotivating them by not achieving absolute success at once.

When to use

As part of quality improvement teams when setting targets and measuring improvement.

How to use

Zero defects is a very simple concept described by Crosby (1984). The process is easy to follow. Using the team approach:

1   Identify and agree the current level of performance.
2   Agree a target and time-scale for the target to be met with milestones.
3   Monitor performance against the target. Publish the results.
4   If the target is met on time recognize the team's performance and repeat from step 2.

Benefits

The use of targets risks demotivating people if they are set in a way that punishes failure rather than recognizes success. Zero defects gives a way of setting tougher targets and recognizing the success of teams that meet them, so encouraging future efforts.

Example

An organization involved in the development of software is experiencing problems with software bugs and is beginning an improvement project to identify the causes of bugs so that the number present in new software releases can be reduced.

The current level of bugs per 1,000 lines of code is 27. The team sets a zero defects target of 15 after the first year. When this is successfully met, the achievement is recognized and the zero defects target for the end of the second year is set as 8. The target is revised every year and the team is recognized for the achievement of the target rather than admonished for the presence of bugs. The targets get tougher in each successive year.

Reference
P.B. Crosby (1984) *Quality without Tears*. New York: McGraw Hill.

ANALYTICAL METHODS

Method 32   Cause and effect analysis

Purpose

To examine effects or problems to find out the possible causes and to point out possible areas where data can be collected.

When to use

When a team is trying to find potential solutions to a problem and is looking for the root cause.

How to use

There are four steps to constructing a cause and effect diagram.

1   Brainstorm all possible causes of the problem or effect selected for analysis.
2   Classify the major causes under the headings: materials, methods, machinery and manpower.
3   Draw a cause and effect diagram (see Figure 1).
4   Write the effects on the diagram under the classifications chosen.

Benefits

When a problem or effect is being analysed, it can be tempting to look for a temporary solution or quick fix that does not solve the problem at all but simply 'gets round' it. Cause and effect analysis allows the problem to be considered fully and all options considered. It also points to possible areas for data collection.

Example

The example shown in Figure 1 examines the possible causes of solder defects on a reflow soldering line. The group looked at all the possible causes and classified them under the main headings as shown. The cause and effect diagram was then used to plan data collection to discover the root cause.

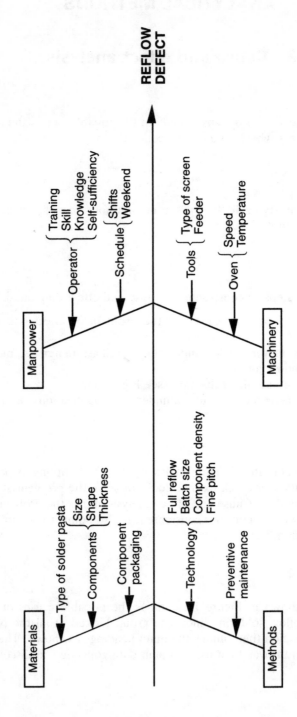

Figure 1 *Cause and effect diagram*

Method 33   Critical path analysis (CPA)

Purpose

A project planning technique which separates the work to be done into discrete elements, allowing the key elements that affect the overall project to be identified.

When to use

At the project design stage and then at all subsequent major project reviews.

How to use

CPA is a very simple process but it can be very time-consuming. To overcome this, there are many software packages available to carry out the computations. Each is different but the basic steps are the same.

1   Brainstorm all of the activities to be carried out and label them.
2   For each activity, record any constraints such as time or order.
3   Draw the flowchart of the activities in time order.
4   Estimate the time for each activity and insert these times in brackets on the appropriate labelled brackets of the network.
5   Using the available software, calculate the critical path and the idle (or float) time left. If the critical path indicates that the project is not possible in the time available, re-examine the assumptions made and modify the finish date if necessary.
6   Monitor progress, recalculating at each review stage, since the changes caused by actual performance can change the critical path.

Benefits

CPA allows the effects of different courses of action to be determined at the planning stage, allowing the best overall approach to be decided.

Example

Smartware Systems Ltd is designing and installing a computer system for a client in the brewing industry. The tasks involved and the estimated duration, together with details of preceding activities which must be completed before

Table 1 *Tasks required to install computer system*

	Activity	Preceding activity	Duration (weeks)
A	Select computer software	–	2
B	Install software	A	3
C	Test software	B	4
D	Develop data base	B	9
E	Install office network	A	2
F	Train employees	C,D	1
G	Test office network	E	6
H	Implement system	F,G	2

a given activity can start, are shown in Table 1. Smartware need to estimate the minimum time taken to complete the project and which activities, if any, have any flexibility for slippage without delaying installation.

Using the network

Network diagrams (Figure 1) are used to control the execution of activities. Some activities will be critical (in that any delay extends the length of the project), while others are not. In big projects, there could be a very large number of activities to consider.

To indicate what spare time there is between activities, we show on the diagram the following information: the event number, for easy reference (top number with circle); the earliest start time for any activity leaving this event (number on left with circle); the latest finish time for any activity entering this event (number on right within circle). The procedure is as follows:

1   Number all the events. Give the start event the number 1 and give the next number to any unnumbered event whose predecessor events are already numbered.

2   Determine the earliest start time (EST) for each event.
    (a)   Set the earliest start time for the start event as zero.
    (b)   For other events, consider the EST of each immediately preceding event and add the duration of the connecting activity. The EST of this new event is the *largest* of these values.

3   Determine the latest finish time (LFT) for each event. These are calculated by working backwards from the finish event.
    (a)   Set the latest finish time of the finish event equal to its earliest start time. This is the target completion time for the project.
    (b)   For other events, consider the LFT of each immediately following event and subtract the duration of the connecting activity. Select the *smallest* of these values.

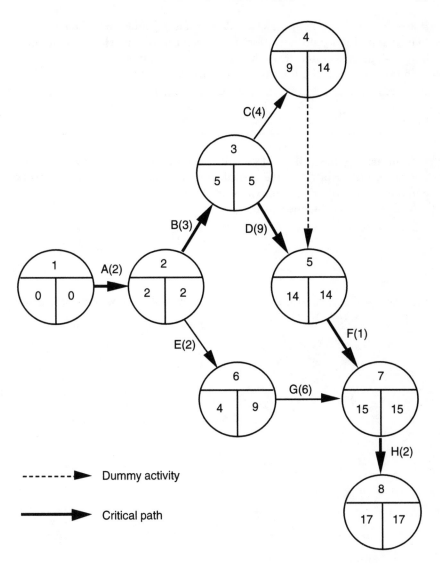

Figure 1   *Network diagram for critical path analysis*

Calculating the float for an activity

The float for a given activity is the extent to which it can be delayed without delaying the project as a whole (assuming all other activities proceed as scheduled). It is calculated as follows:

$$\text{Float} = \frac{\text{latest finish time of}}{\text{following event}} - \text{duration} - \frac{\text{earliest start time of}}{\text{preceding event}}$$

If any activity has a float of, say, 3 days, then if it took up to 3 days longer than planned it would not affect the project duration. However, a delay longer than this *would* delay the project's completion.

In our example, the float for each activity is as follows:

Activity	A	B	C	D	E	F	G	H
Float	0	0	5	0	5	0	5	0

If an activity has a float of zero it is a critical activity. Any delay in a critical activity will delay the overall project. Paths through the network composed only of critical activities are known as *critical paths*.

The critical path is therefore:

$$A \rightarrow B \rightarrow D \rightarrow F \rightarrow H$$

Reference

D.R. Anderson, D.J. Sweeney and T.A. Williams (1994) *An Introduction to Management Sciences*. New York: West.

Method 34 Departmental cost of quality

Purpose

To provide a financial measure of the quality performance of an organization.

When to use

Either at the beginning of a total quality process to establish the need for change or later when identifying opportunities for improvement.

How to use

Departmental cost of quality identifies three specific cost areas:

1 *Prevention* The cost associated with planning, training and writing procedures associated with doing it right first time.
2 *Appraisal* The cost of checking and testing to find out whether it has been done right first time.
3 *Failure* The cost, internal or external, associated with failure to do it right first time.

These costs are calculated in two distinct ways. First, the *hard*, or accounts, costs in each category:

1 *Prevention* e.g. training courses, preventive maintenance.
2 *Appraisal* e.g. depreciation of test equipment and inspection contracts.
3 *Failure* e.g. scrap, re-work, warranty.

All of these costs are directly identified from accounts information.
Secondly, the *soft*, or people, costs in each category:

1 *Prevention* e.g. percentage of people's time spent on training, writing procedures, planning etc.
2 *Appraisal* e.g. percentage of people's time spent on checking, testing etc.
3 *Failure* e.g. percentage of people's time spent on re-work, handling failure in all its forms.

All of these are estimated either directly or as part of an estimate including normal work (see Table 1). These estimates are then converted to cost by using average departmental cost figures from accounts.

Benefits

Identifying the departmental cost of quality in an organization can have several benefits:

Table 1 *Cost of quality estimate*

Work description	Time spent (%)	Portion of time Normal work	P	A	F	Cost of quality Normal work	P	A	F
Receipt and banking of cheques	5	100				5			
Posting cash receipts to sales ledger	15	100				15			
Process credit notes from RCRs received for returned goods, price adjustments, new delay, etc.	15				100				15
Chase payment of overdue DRs using phone/letter/fax etc.	20				100				20
Check statements at end of month and highlight overdue sums, export, recent payments etc.	5			100				5	
Review picking notes rec A/Cs on hold and inform supplier of situation	5			100				5	
Deal with customer enquiries re. copy invoices. Now deliver and supply the required info.	35				100				35
Total	100					20	–	10	70

P, prevention; A, appraisal; F, failure.

Source: Kanji and Asher, 1993

1 It provides a benchmark for future performance.
2 It builds individual and company-wide awareness of the importance of quality.
3 It identifies improvement projects for action.
4 It identifies areas for investment in quality.
5 It allows departments to chart progress in cost terms.

Example

The cost of quality was estimated in an accounts department, where estimates were made of normal work, prevention, appraisal and failure (see Table 1).

References

BS 6143: *Guide to the Economics of Quality*.
G.W. Parker (1992) *Achieving Cost Efficient Quality*. London: Gower.

Method 35   Domainal mapping

Purpose

To assist in the identification of internal customers and their needs.

When to use

Either during the diagnostic phase of a total quality process when conducting internal interviews or as part of a departmental purpose analysis when reviewing the internal customer–supplier relationship.

How to use

Begin the process by drawing a circle and placing yourself or your department in the centre of the circle. Spokes are drawn out from the centre representing different internal customers and a circle is drawn at the end of each spoke. The names of the internal customers are written in each circle.

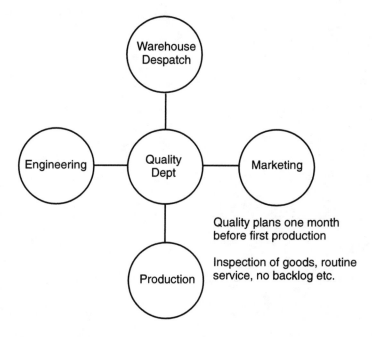

Figure 1   *Domainal mapping*

For each internal customer, write down on the spoke what you believe that their requirements are. When this is complete, visit each customer in turn and agree or alter the requirements. Then agree how the requirement will be measured and how feedback of performance will be given.

Benefits

Domainal mapping gives a pictorial representation that allows you to think through internal relationships and the requirements and measures that go with them.

Example

Figure 1 shows a domainal map drawn by a quality manager establishing his links with other departments in the organization. The Quality Department identifies its requirements, i.e. goods inspection, routine service and no backlog etc., from the Production Department. The requirements will be measured and feedback of performance will be given in order to fulfil the needs of internal customers.

Method 36   Evolutionary operation (EVOP)

Purpose

A sequential experimental procedure for collecting information during on-line production to improve a process without disturbing output.

When to use

When off-line experimentation is expensive and you would like to use on-line process control. It should be run not only to produce product but also to provide information on how to improve the process and product.

How to use

It requires a simple two-stage process using simple statistical concepts. It is run during normal routine production by plant personnel. At each stage a simple design is used to estimate the direction of increase or decrease of the yield as required by the experiment. Through the planned introduction of minor variants into the process, the operating conditions are made.

Proceeding a certain step-length in the required direction, lay down a second experiment to re-estimate the increase until there is no further improvement. Constant repetition of this programme will lead to continual improvement of the process.

Benefits

It provides sequential searching of the design space for the improvement of the process without disturbing production.

Example

In an industrial process, two temperatures are identified as having an effect on the percentage of parts with no faults. The two temperatures are surface temperature (t_1) and base temperature (t_2). The first experiment gave the following results:

t_1^0	t_2^0	Yield in percentage
740	250	56
750	270	56
740	270	71
750	250	70
745	260	68

To estimate the direction of increase, the fitted linear model of the process from the first experiment was:

$$Y = 68.2 + 0.950 \, (t_1 - 745) + 0.525 \, (t_2 - 260)$$

The centre for the second experiment was taken at (765, 275) and the results were:

t_1^0	t_2^0	Yield in percentage
760	270	80
770	280	97
760	280	95
770	270	96
765	275	94

The above information indicates that the improvement on the percentage yield can be obtained by using $t_1^0 = 770$ and $t_2^0 = 280$. Repetition of this procedure will lead to the optimum improvement of the process.

Reference

Thomas D. Barker (1994) Quality by Experimental Design. New York: Marcel Dekker.

Method 37 Failure mode and effect analysis (FMEA)

Purpose

To assist in the foolproofing of a design or a process.

When to use

When investigating a process to identify possible causes of failure, or when examining a product or service to look for what *can* go wrong. In the latter case, FMEA takes place at the design stage to allow prevention to be 'planned in'.

How to use

FMEA offers a structure for thinking through the likelihood, seriousness and probability of detection of potential problems. There is a simple process to be followed:

1 Brainstorm what can go wrong. A list of potential problems is generated, offering as many difficulties as possible.
2 For each potential problem, estimate how likely it is to be found if it is wrong. This is graded on a scale of 1–10 as follows:

Scale	Interpretation	Probability of detection (%)
1	Very high	86–100
2	Very high	76–85
3	High	66–75
4	High	56–65
5	Moderate	46–55
6	Moderate	36–45
7	Low	26–35
8	Low	16–25
9	Very low	6–15
10	Remote	0–5

3 For each potential problem, estimate how costly it is likely to be. This is graded on a scale of 1–10 as follows:

Scale	Interpretation
1	Minor
2	Low
3	Low
4	Moderate
5	Moderate
6	Moderate
7	High
8	High
9	Very high
10	Catastrophic

4   Estimate how likely it is that each potential failure will happen. A scale of 1–10 is used as before:

Scale	Interpretation	Likelihood
1	Remote	Effectively 0
2	Very low	1 in 20,000
3	Low	1 in 10,000
4	Moderate	1 in 2,000
5	Moderate	1 in 1,000
6	Moderate	1 in 200
7	High	1 in 100
8	High	1 in 20
9	Very high	1 in 10
10	Very high	1 in 2

5   Multiply the outputs from stages 2, 3 and 4 together to generate a risk priority number (RPN). The RPN will lie between 1 and 10,000. If each stage gave a result of 5 the RPN would be 125.

6   Rank the potential by the RPN. Two rules are then used. First, no potential failure can have an RPN of greater than 700; secondly, no individual output from stages 2, 3 or 4 can exceed 7. These rules show which potential failures must be investigated.

Benefits

Failure mode and effect analysis gives a structured way of assessing possible failures and which areas to investigate first. A major advantage is that it does this at an early stage in both products and processes.

Example

A company making plastic mouldings was examining a new process: the hot water annealing of nylon injection-moulded components. Two possible

Component no: VARIOUS

Component description: VARIOUS NYLON INJECTION MOULDINGS   Supplier/Unit name(s): MOULDING/ANNEALING DEPT   Site: BASINGSTOKE

Project: NYLON ANNEALING   Engineer responsible: B G CHAPMAN

FMEA date (original): APRIL 92   (Latest revision): ....

Occurrence: High no.—Likely / Low no.—Unlikely
Severity: High no.—High severity / Low no.—Low severity
Detection: High no.—Unlikely to detect / Low no.—Likely to detect

Item no.	Process function	Potential failure mode	Effect(s) of failure	Cause(s) of failure	Current controls	Existing conditions Occurrence	Severity	Detection	Risk priority number (RPN)	Recommended action(s) and status	Responsible Area/Engineer for corrective action	Action(s) taken	Revised conditions Occurrence	Severity	Detection	Risk priority number (RPN)
P20	Hot water annealing of nylon injection moulded components															
1		Under anneal/ Over anneal	(a) Parts difficult to assemble (b) Parts brittle time caused break drive installation (c) Parts fail prematurely in use (d) Parts too flexible for installation (e) Parts do not provide function when fitted	(i) Missed op	Work instruction box label mark Xs	1	8	3	24	No action needed						
				(ii) Insufficient process time caused by: (a) Inadequate control data or out of date information	Irregular periodic issue of control data	4	8	4	128	(a) Arrange for weekly update/ issue of control data retrieval of obsolete files (b) Supervisor checks instal. + log errors	Data processing / S Pearson	Weekly batch run of control data Implemented Aug 92 Hourly supervisor checks log book installed Aug 92 (a) Numeric clock/ siren/light fitted Aug 92	1	8	4	32
				(b) Operator failing to start/stop press to time (c) Instal. digital clock conditions sheet + visual or mis-reading clock	Verbal interaction + control data operator attention	3	8	4	128	(a) Instal. digital clock + audible alarm + flashing light (b) Instal automatic lid releaser basket lift open	Maintenance	clock start on lid close (b) Auto basket release fitted Sept 92	1	8	1	8

Component no: VARIOUS

Figure 1 *Failure mode and effect analysis*

Source: Kanji and Asher, 1993

Component no: VARIOUS

Component description: VARIOUS NYLON INJECTION MOULDINGS

Project: NYLON ANNEALING

Supplier/Unit name(s): MOULDING/ANNEALING DEPT

Site: BASINGSTOKE

Engineer responsible: B G CHAPMAN

FMEA date (original): APRIL 92

(Latest revision): ....

Sheet 2 of 2

Occurrence: High no.—Likely / Low no.—Unlikely

Severity: High no.—High severity / Low no.— Low severity

Detection: High no.—Unlikely to detect / Low no.—Likely to detect

Item no.	Process function	Potential failure mode	Effect(s) of failure	Cause(s) of failure	Current controls	Occurrence	Severity	Detection	Risk priority number (RPN)	Recommended action(s) and status	Responsible Area/Engineer for corrective action	Action(s) taken	Occurrence	Severity	Detection	Risk priority number (RPN)
							Existing conditions							Revised conditions		
1 Cont'd		Under anneal	As page 1	(iii) Incorrect water temperature caused by:												
				(a) Immersion of cold product dropping water temp.	Operator instruct	5	8	5	200	Line water temp. controller to start digital clock upon reaching correct temp.	Maintenance	Temp. controller linked to digital clock Aug 92	1	8	5	40
				(b) Cold water top up employed to cover for water dragout dripping tank temp.	Operator Resp.	5	8	5	200	Fit hot water auto top-up + temp. controller to start clock	Maintenance	Auto hot water top-up facility fitted Sept 92	1	8	5	40
				(iv) Excessive annealing times used	See (ii) a&b	4	4	8	128	As per (ii) a&b	Maintenance	Aug/Sept 92	1	1	8	8
				(v) Poly bag not sealed adequately	Bag scaler W/I	2	2	8	32	No action	—	—				
				(vi) Poly bag punctures due to sharp products	Mat'l selection of poly bag laminate	3	3	8	168	Upgrade poly bag laminate specification	Design Eng.	New heavy duty laminate specified June 92	1	7	8	56

Component no: VARIOUS

Figure 1 Continued

failure modes were identified as under/over-annealing, and the effects of the failure were identified. As a result of the study (Figure 1), areas with high RPNs were examined and actions to prevent these occurring were put into place. The RPNs were recalculated under revised conditions and showed a dramatic fall.

Reference

G. McAndrew and S. O'Sullivan (1993) *FMEAs: a Manager's Handbook.* London: Stanley Thornes.

Method 38   Fault tree analysis

Purpose

To perform a quantitative as well as qualitative analysis of a complex system.

When to use

When you want to illustrate the connection between a non-desired occurrence on the system level and the causes of this occurrence on a lower system level.

How to use

Design of the fault tree begins by specifying the non-desired occurrence. The immediate cause of this event then has to be connected with the necessary sequence. This procedure is repeated until a basic fault occurrence level is reached.

Benefits

It helps to increase understanding of the formation and reliability of the system. It also helps to detect critical failure modes even when the component data are not available.

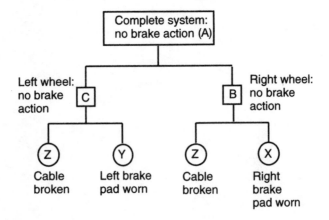

Figure 1   *Fault tree analysis*

Example

In a handbrake system consider the failures 'brake pad worn' and 'cable broken' with the following notation.

A   Complete system: no brake action
B   Right wheel: no brake action
C   Left wheel: no brake action
X   Right brake pad worn
Y   Left brake pad worn
Z   Cable broken

The fault tree analysis for the occurrence of factor A is shown in Figure 1.

Reference

B. Bergman and B. Klefsjo (1994) *Quality from Customer Needs to Customer Satisfaction.* New York: McGraw-Hill.

Method 39   Force field analysis

Purpose

Allows you to identify those forces that both help and hinder you in closing the gap between where you are now and where you want to be.

When to use

When a team is planning to implement a solution or make a major change.

How to use

There are seven simple steps involved in force field analysis:

1   Identify the current situation. This is likely to reflect the problem statement. Place this statement in the centre at the top of a page. Below the statement draw a vertical line to the bottom of the page.
2   Identify where you should be: the desired state. This is placed on the right-hand side of the page at the top. Again, draw a vertical line to the bottom. The aim is to move the centre line to the right-hand side, moving from the current situation to where you want to be.
3   Brainstorm all the aspects that help: these forces move the line to the right (positive forces).
4   Brainstorm all the forces that hinder: these forces move the line to the left (negative forces).
5   Estimate the ease of increasing helping forces and decreasing hindering forces on a scale of 1–5 as follows: 5, very easy; 4, easy; 3, medium; 2, difficult; 1, very difficult.
6   Estimate the impact of helping and hindering forces, again using a scale of 1–5 as follows: 5, very strong; 4, strong; 3, medium; 2, low; 1, very weak.
7   Work out the priority number of each force by multiplying (5) by (6).

Benefits

Force field analysis allows a team to think through the effect of changes, identify which forces have most impact, and see where effort can be used to maximum effect.

Example

An organization in the uniformed services is considering implementing a major cultural change process and used force field analysis to assist in its

	Ease of change	Impact	Total	+ Forces (Helping) → ← − Forces (Hindering)		Ease of change	Impact	Total
	3	3	6	Communication	Fear for future	2	3	5
	2	2	4	Training	Lack of trust	2	3	5
	3	3	6	Employees' desire to be involved	Poor coordination	2	2	4
	2	3	5	Competition/CCT	Unionized managers	2	3	5
					Lack of confidence	2	2	4

Figure 1 *Positive and negative forces in force field analysis*

introduction. Figure 1 clearly identifies the positive and negative forces at work and helps the management team to plan the introduction of the change. The team decided to concentrate heavily on the communication of the changes, in such a way as to build trust in the organization's future.

Reference

R. Chang and M. Niedzwiecki (1993) *Continuous Improvement Tools*. California: Richard Chang.

Method 40 Minute analysis

Purpose

To estimate the survival period of a particular product unit under certain conditions, using a simulated experimental environment.

When to use

When the duration of the testing period is predetermined and some of the test units could survive the duration of the experiment. In general, the resulting data are expressed in the continuous mode with the specification of a failure or a survival for the whole testing period. Such an analysis requires the assumption of the failure distribution of the unit. A method for minute analysis does not require such an assumption.

How to use

In a testing experiment, first break down the test period into regular intervals of a specific duration called *minimum units* ('minutes'). The duration of the minimum unit depends on the problem under investigation. An experiment was conducted to investigate in which minimum unit the end of the life of a unit took place. The data are used in binary form with '1' ('0') signifying that the test unit will still be functioning (not functioning) by the end of a particular cycle. The analysis of variance technique is performed in the usual way appropriate for binary data.

Benefits

It does not require the assumption that the failure distribution of the unit follows a complicated (Weibull-type) probability distribution.

Examples

In order to improve the durability of fluorescent lamps, the following factors were selected for study:

A Additive (2 types)
B Fluorescent agents (2 types)
C Coating method (2 types)
D Tube-washing method (2 types)

For each of the eight combinations, the durability of two lamps was tested. The whole testing period was ten days. Every two days, how many lamps were still functioning was recorded. An analysis of variance table can be constructed using the data from this experiment.

To determine the best operating conditions for the paper-feeding phase at high speed of an off-set duplicator, the following four factors at two levels were selected.

Description	Level
Vacuum header type	Normal
	Light weight
Feed can type	Normal
	Smoothed
Master cylinder can	Smoothed
	Normal
Air rifle selling	Normal
	High

The data will represent the number of paper sheets successfully fed through the duplicator at each test.

After statistical analysis for each of the eight levels, the best operating conditions for paper feeding can be obtained.

Reference

N. Logothetis and H. Wynn (1991) *Quality through Design*. Oxford: Oxford Science Publications.

Method 41   Paired comparisons

Purpose

To help a group to quantify the preferences of its members.

When to use

At the end of a brainstorming session, when trying to reduce a list to manageable size.

How to use

Each option is compared head to head with every other option. In each instance, each member of the group is asked to vote for one or other of the options. The number of votes for each option is then totalled and the option with the most votes is chosen.

The steps to do this are simple:

1 Set up a grid as shown in Table 1 below. The number of possible comparisons depends upon the number of options.
2 Each member has one and only one vote in each comparison.
3 Everyone must vote in each comparison, however unappealing.

Benefits

Paired comparisons force a group to reach a single conclusion. Sometimes, as a result, the group is dissatisfied with the conclusion and votes again.

Table 1 *Paired comparisons of desirable school features*

Options	Av.B	Av.C	Av.D	Av.E	Bv.C	Bv.D	Bv.E	Cv.D	Cv.E	Dv.E	Totals
A	5	7	8	5							25
B	3				6	5	7				21
C		1			2			4	5		12
D			0			3		4		5	12
E				3			1		3	3	10

Example

A group of eight sixth-form pupils have brainstormed a list of characteristics desirable in a school. These are:

A Understanding the relevance of lessons
B Respect for teachers
C Good facilities
D Fair rules
E Extra-curricular activities

The results of paired comparisons are given in Table 1. The most important feature, from the pupils' viewpoint, is understanding the relevance of lessons.

Reference

P. Spenley (1992) *World Class Performance through Total Quality*. London: Chapman and Hall.

Method 42   Parameter design

Purpose

To determine which factors are important in the manufacturing process and to find the optimum set of working conditions.

When to use

When you want to reduce the variability of a process by changing the variability-control factors, while maintaining the required average performance through appropriate adjustments to the target-control factors.

How to use

Suppose that we have three components in our process and that we decide to look at two stages of each component. We then use all eight possible combinations and make four runs at each of the eight ($2^3 = 8$) combinations. We can analyse the data in two ways. First, we take as the response the mean of the sets of observations. In the second analysis, we take as the performance characteristic the estimated variance at each of the eight combinations.

Benefits

It can provide the means both to reduce costs and improve quality. By making effective use of experimental design and statistical techniques, one can identify the settings of easy-to-control product or process parameters.

Example

Consider an electrical power circuit where the characteristic of interest is the output voltage with a target value of y_0. Assume that the voltage is largely determined by the gain of a transistor in the circuit whose nominal value (x) can be controlled. Suppose that the effect of the transistor gain on the output voltage is non-linear. A transistor with a gain of x_0 would produce the required output voltage of y_0. The effect of a variation about the nominal value x_0 on the resulting variation about y_0 is indicated by bands straddling the nominal values. However, if the circuit designer chooses a nominal gain of x, then, owing to the non-linearity of response, it can be seen that the variation about the corresponding voltage, y, is much reduced. Now suppose that there is a resistor in the circuit which has a linear effect on the voltage at all levels of transistor gain, then the resistance of this component can be chosen so that the difference between the voltage, y, and the desired voltage y_0 is eliminated. The response is then on target and the variability in response is minimized. Thus transistor gain is a variability-control factor and resistance is a target-control factor.

Reference

P.W.M. John (1990) *Statistical Methods in Engineering and Quality Assurance*. New York: Wiley.

Method 43   Process cost of quality

Purpose

To provide a financial measure of the quality performance of an organization.

When to use

Either at the beginning of a total quality process to establish the need for change or later when identifying opportunities for improvement.

How to use

Process cost of quality identifies two specific cost areas:

1 *Conformance*   The cost associated with planning, training and writing procedures associated with doing it right first time, together with the cost of checking and testing to find out whether it has been done right first time. These are the costs of operating the process as it is in a wholly effective manner (the concern is *not* whether the process is necessary or efficient). This means that when operated as specified, it cannot be done at lower cost. The *Cost of conformance* is the minimum cost for the process as specified.
2 *Non-conformance*   The cost, internal or external, associated with inefficiency in the process.

These costs are calculated in two distinct ways. First, the *hard*, or accounts, costs in each category:

1 *Conformance* e.g. training courses, preventive maintenance, depreciation of test equipment and inspection contracts, together with the normal costs associated with the process.
2 *Non-conformance* e.g. scrap, re-work, warranty.

All of these costs are directly identified from accounts information.
Secondly, the *soft*, or people, costs in each category:

1 *Conformance* e.g. percentage of people's time spent on training, writing, planning, checking, testing etc.
2 *Non-conformance* e.g. percentage of people's time spent on re-work, handling failure in all its forms.

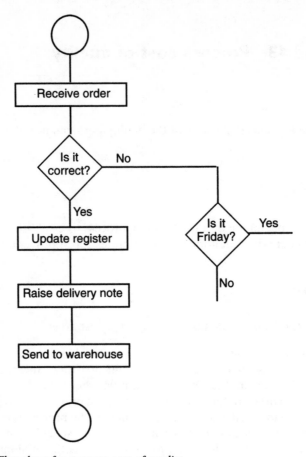

Figure 1   *Flowchart for process cost of quality*

All of these are estimated either directly or as part of an estimate including normal work. These estimates are then converted to cost by using average departmental cost figures from accounts. Process cost reduction can come from two distinct areas: reduction in CONC (cost of non-conformance) via operators and reduction in COC (cost of conformance) via process owners.

Benefits

Identifying the process cost of quality in an organization can have several benefits:

1   It provides a benchmark for future performance.
2   It builds individual and company-wide awareness of the importance of quality and inter-departmental issues.
3   It identifies improvement projects for action.
4   It identifies areas for investment in quality.

Example

The flowchart showing how a sales department receives and processes orders is shown in Figure 1. The costs of conformance include:

- receiving the order
- checking the order for correctness and authorization
- updating the control register
- raising the delivery note
- sending the note to the warehouse

The costs of non-conformance include:

- returning incorrect invoices
- returning outstanding orders
- answering telephone queries
- dealing with resubmitted orders.

References

BS 6143: *Guide to the Economics of Quality*.
B.G. Dale and J.J. Plunkett (1991) *Quality Costing*. London: Chapman and Hall.

Method 44   Reliability

Purpose

To find the cause of failures and try to eliminate them and to reduce the effects or consequences of failure.

When to use

When the intrinsic characteristic of an object, system or function is not performing as expected by its user for the period of time intended by the designer of the object or system.

How to use

Study a unit randomly chosen from a manufactured batch. The probability that this unit will work after the operating time t can be estimated by measuring the mean time to failure of the unit. This can be achieved by obtaining the times to failure for many units of the same kind operating under the same conditions. This probability, regarded as a function of t, is called the reliability function and is written $R(t)$. If $R(1000) = 0.99$, this implies that about 99 per cent of the units of a batch will survive 1,000 operating hours.

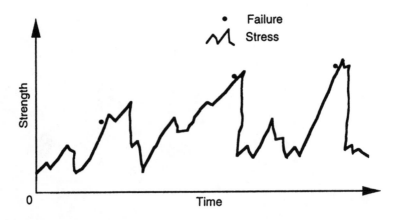

Figure 1   *Reliability diagram*

Benefits

It helps to increase the failure resistance of the product and the tolerance of the product to failures.

Example

In a stress–strength analysis experiment it was observed that many failures happened due to a weak point, which had been exposed to a strong stress. This stress can arise due to external or internal conditions. Gradual weakening can be caused by fatigue, corrosion, deterioration or diffusion. The catastrophic effect is, as a rule, an immediate overload. Figure 1 indicates the effects of stress on a unit.

Reference

B. Bergman and B. Klefsjo (1994) *Quality: from Customer Needs to Customer Satisfaction.* New York: McGraw-Hill.

Method 45   Robust design (off-line quality control)

Purpose

To achieve the proper functioning of a component even when affected by interfering factors, whether external, internal or manufacturing variation.

When to use

When the individual unit of a product is exposed to disturbance and to focus on reducing the variability of the process.

How to use

Divide the disturbing factors into the following groups:
1 *Inner disturbances*, i.e. wear and tear of the individual unit due to its operation.
2 *Outer disturbances*, i.e. variation of temperature and other environmental factors during usage.
3 *Manufacturing variation*, i.e. deviation from the set target.

   Use the design to check whether individual units exposed to the above disturbances alter or vary in important characteristics.

Benefits

It helps to focus on reducing the variability of the process by designing quality into the process.

Example

Statisticians use the term 'robust' to mean insensitive to departures from set conditions. The sample median can be preferred to the sample mean as an estimator because it is robust against extreme observations.

   It is often possible to choose a design that will be more or less sensitive to disturbance. In an experiment, the amplification of a transistor and the output of voltage can be adopted following the design process. By choosing a nominal amplification A_1 instead of A_0, the voltage can be adjusted by the spread of actual amplification. The level can then be controlled towards the target value with the help of a resistor.

Reference

B. Bergman and B. Klefsjo (1994) *Quality: From Customer Needs to Customer Satisfaction.* New York: McGraw-Hill.

Method 46 Solution effect analysis

Purpose

To examine solutions to problems to find out whether there are any detrimental consequences and to plan the implementation of the solution.

When to use

When a team has found potential solutions to a problem and is examining them to decide which to implement.

How to use

There are four steps to constructing a solution effect diagram.

1 Brainstorm all possible effects of the solution selected for analysis.
2 Classify the effects under the headings: materials, methods, equipment and people.
3 Draw a solution effect diagram (see Figure 1).
4 Write the effects on the diagram under the classifications chosen.

Benefits

A proposed beneficial change may have side-effects elsewhere. These side-effects may be as bad as the problem being solved. Solution effect analysis allows the implementation of change to be planned by identifying and removing any detrimental side-effects.

Example

The example shown in Figure 1 examines the effects of introducing a new working method into an office. The group looked at all the possible effects of a new accounting system, and classified them under the main headings as shown.

The solution effect diagram was then used to plan the introduction and minimize the side-effects of the new method. This was done by taking each item off the solution effect diagram in turn – for example, 'remove old

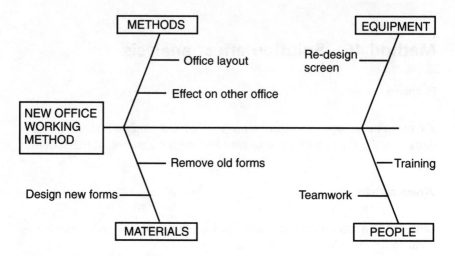

Figure 1 *Solution effect diagram*

forms' – and agreeing a plan with users and a time-scale to bring about the necessary action. The result was minimum disruption.

Method 47   Stratification

Purpose

To assist in the definition of a problem by identifying where it does and does not occur.

When to use

In teams, when trying to identify a problem and define it precisely as the first stage of problem-solving.

How to use

Stratification is a method of splitting data according to whether it does or does not meet a set of criteria. The value of the technique is to expose patterns in the data. It is used *before* data collection begins to design the way in which data will be collected, and *after* data collection as a way of focusing the analysis.

The process is very simple.

1   Brainstorm a list of criteria or characteristics that could cause systematic differences in the data. These are not necessarily things that *do* cause differences but things that *could* cause them.
2   Design the data collection forms to include these items.
3   Collect the data and examine them for any patterns or trends.

Benefits

By focusing on data before collection, stratification ensures that all necessary data are collected first time and avoids wasted effort.

Example

A team was examining the problem of absenteeism. The list of characteristics generated at the start was:

Name
Age
Sex
Day
Consecutive days

Month
Boss name
Work area
Overtime worked
Total days absent

The data collected were analysed according to these categories and patterns looked for. Analysts might, for example, reveal that the day after pay day or certain days of the month were particularly prone to absenteeism.

Reference

B. Bergman and B. Klefsjo (1994) *Quality: from Customer Needs to Customer Satisfaction*. New York: McGraw-Hill.

Method 48   System design

Purpose

To apply special scientific and engineering knowledge to produce a basic functional prototype model, having surveyed the relevant technology, manufacturing environment and customer need.

When to use

To design quality into the process by carrying out research and development experiments in order to find the best operating conditions for the satisfaction of the customer.

How to use

Reject the notion that to be outside specification is bad, but to be within specification, even by only a whisker, is satisfactory. Replace it by the new idea of process capability in connection with the criteria C_p and C_{pk}. Make people think in terms of aiming for a target value and work to reduce the mean square error that is the sum of the square of the bias and the variance. It is necessary to control both of them because the process requires zero bias and smallest possible variance.

Benefits

It helps to take the prototype model and make it happen according to customer requirements.

Example

The process capability index C_p is

$$C_p = \frac{\text{USL}-\text{LSL}}{6\sigma} - \frac{2\delta}{6\sigma}$$

When USL and LSL are the upper and lower specification limits respectively. As σ (standard deviation) decreases, C_p increases. 2δ is specification width.

The second criterion is

$$C_{pk} = \text{minimum (CPL, CPU)} = C_p(1-k)$$

when

$$\text{CPU} = \frac{\text{USL}-\mu}{3\sigma}, \text{CPL} = \frac{\mu-\text{LSL}}{3\sigma}, \text{and } k = \frac{|\mu_0-\mu|}{\delta}$$

where μ_0 = target value, μ = actual average, CPU = upper process capability and CPL = lower process capability.

Nowadays, semiconductor manufacturers are striving for processes with $C_p = 2.0$ and $C_{pk} = 1.5$ which represents about 3.4 defective parts per million.

Reference

P.W.M. John (1990) *Statistical Methods in Engineering and Quality Assurance*. New York: Wiley.

Method 49   Taguchi methods

Purpose

A technique for the optimization of products or processes, Taguchi involves a two-stage experimental design that gives the benefits of robustness and efficiency with the minimum number of experiments.

When to use

During design, commissioning or post-commissioning when seeking the optimum operating characteristics of a product or process.

How to use

Experimental design usually involves attempting to optimize a process which can involve several factors (e.g., temperature, time, chemical composition) at several levels (e.g., five possible temperatures, four possible times, six possible chemical compositions). Factors can also be attributes; for example, a switch can be on or off.

The factorial approach to experimental design would thus involve $6 \times 4 \times 5$ cells $\times$ the replications needed for accuracy. This is a minimum of 120 experiments and could, depending on the variability, be 360 or more. This can in practice be reduced by what are known as fractional factorial designs but the number is still large.

The Taguchi approach takes each of the factors at two levels (usually the extremes) and works out which has the greatest contribution to the end result. These factors are then studied in more detail. In our example, the experiment would probably involve studying three factors in eight experiments with one repeat, so that the initial design would involve 16 experiments as compared with a possible 360. This design would allow all the factors and their interactions to be estimated.

Designs of this type were originally developed by Plackett and Burmann in the UK and tables are available giving many different designs together with analysis details. The designs are in the form of matrices called orthogonal arrays.

The stages to go through are:

1   Selection of the factors and/or interactions to be evaluated.
2   Selection of the number of levels of the factors.
3   Selection of the appropriate orthogonal array.
4   Assignment of the factors or interactions to the columns.

Table 1 *Orthogonal array resulting from paper manufacture experiments*

| | Factor | | | | | | | Waste |
Trial no.	A	B	C	D	E	F	G	(%)
1	1	1	1	1	1	1	1	12
2	1	1	1	2	2	2	2	15
3	1	2	2	1	1	2	2	13
4	1	2	2	2	2	1	1	9
5	2	1	2	1	2	1	2	8
6	2	1	2	2	1	2	1	22
7	2	2	1	1	2	2	1	20
8	2	2	1	2	1	1	2	26

5   Conduct the experiment.
6   Analyse the results.
7   Carry out a confirmation experiment.

Benefits

Taguchi methods give a fast and pragmatic approach to the optimization of products and processes. They can also be used for tolerance design: the setting of statistically based tolerances, allowing either improved performance through tighter tolerances or cheaper designs in non-critical areas; and for fast type approval testing.

Example

A company involved in paper manufacture was seeking to optimize the process in terms of grade 1 output. The parameters thought to have influence were:

Factor A	Machine speed	55ft/s	60 ft/s
Factor B	Coating	0.2mm	0.18mm
Factor C	Wire position	High	Low
Factor D	Clay content	High	Low

A decision was taken to carry out a seven-factor-in-eight experiment design, using the remaining four factors to represent interactions between the major factors. The orthogonal array is given in Table 1.

The total waste for:

$$A1 \text{ was } (12 + 15 + 13 + 9)/4 = 49/4 = 12.25\%$$
$$A2 \text{ was } (8 + 22 + 20 + 26)/4 = 76/4 = 19.0\%$$

$$B1 \text{ was } (12 + 15 + 8 + 22)/4 = 57/4 = 14.25\%$$
$$B2 \text{ was } (13 + 9 + 20 + 26)/4 = 68/4 = 17.00\%$$

C1 was $(12 + 15 + 20 + 26)/4 = 73/4 = 18.25\%$
C2 was $(13 + 9 + 8 + 22)/4 = 52/4 = 13.00\%$

D1 was $(12 + 13 + 8 + 20)/4 = 53/4 = 13.25\%$
D2 was $(15 + 9 + 22 + 26)/4 = 72/4 = 18.00\%$

Machine speed was seen to be the major factor and the optimum operating condition was forecast to be

A1   B1   C2   D1

Which was later confirmed by experiment.

Reference

P.J. Ross (1988) *Taguchi Techniques for Quality Engineering*. New York: McGraw-Hill.

Method 50   Tolerance design

Purpose

To find out by experiment where the variability in a process (product) occurs and where adjustments can be made.

When to use

When the influences of inner and outer sources of 'noise' cannot be successfully reduced by use of *parameter design* (Method 42). Here 'noise' represents the effects of uncontrollable factors.

How to use

It requires the same steps as parameter design, but additional factors are considered that were previously excluded because of cost or the difficulty of experimentation.

If this also fails, the tolerance of the product's components are considered. This means retaining the optimum nominal levels of actors, but reducing the tolerance of certain crucial factors in an optimal and cost-effective way so that overall variability in the response is reduced to acceptable levels.

Benefits

It assists in the study of factors which are expensive and difficult to change in experiments for the improvement of a process.

Example

If we run a second outer array centered on the optimum parameter conditions, this time the noise factors are noise in the parts themselves. If factor A is a resistor at a nominal level of 100 ohms, it becomes, in the noise array, a factor with levels of, say, 100 ± 2. When the array has been run, we find how much variability is associated with each factor and, hence, where we have to make further improvements.

Reference

P.W.M. John (1990) *Statistical Methods in Engineering and Quality Assurance*. New York: Wiley.

IDEA GENERATION

Method 51   Brainstorming

Purpose

To generate as many ideas as possible without assessing their value.

When to use

In teams, when trying to identify possible root causes or when seeking solutions to a problem. Brainstorming can also be used when deciding what problem or improvement activity to work on, and when planning the steps of a project.

How to use

Brainstorming seems very simple. It works best when the team meeting is informal. To help this there are eight basic rules:

1   Keep the meeting relaxed.
2   Select a leader to write the ideas on a flip chart.
3   Involve the right people in the team.
4   Define the problem clearly. You will need to check that everyone present has the same understanding of the problem. This can be difficult to achieve in practice. A useful first stage of any brainstorm could involve a brief discussion of the problem before a definition is agreed.
5   Generate as many ideas as possible without discussion or evaluation. This comes later. There are two main ways of doing this. The first is simply to invite people to contribute and write the ideas down as they are suggested. This is called the 'free wheeling' method. The second is to go round the room asking each person in turn for his or her contribution. This is called the 'round robin' method.
6   Encourage everyone to contribute. This is best done by beginning the session with a trivial example, such as 'uses of a paper cup', to get everyone started before moving on to the question in hand.
7   Write down every idea. There should be no censorship and there is no such thing as a bad idea. Sometimes strange ideas open up a new area of thought.
8   Following the brainstorm, a technique such as list reduction (Method 59) should be used to reduce the brainstormed list to manageable proportions.

Benefits

By encouraging everyone to contribute, brainstorming breaks down barriers between departments and levels of hierarchy. It therefore allows everyone to contribute equally to the team. Brainstorming encourages cooperative and collaborative behaviour and is also useful in the development of groupwork skills.

Remember that brainstorming involves collecting people's ideas and opinions and that it might be necessary to collect data following the brainstorm to allow any decisions to be taken on the basis of fact.

Example

An organization was seeking suggestions to reduce absenteeism. They ran a series of brainstorming sessions to generate ideas for tackling the problem.

Reference

R. Chang and M. Niedzwiecki (1993) *Continuous Improvement Tools*. California: Richard Chang.

Method 52   Brainwriting

Purpose

To generate as many ideas as possible.

When to use

In teams, when trying to identify possible root causes or when seeking solutions to a problem. Whereas brainstorming generates as many ideas as possible, brainwriting results in fewer, but more fully developed, ideas.

How to use

The success of brainwriting depends upon having an agreed definition of the problem to be addressed before beginning the session. This should be checked with all team members before the start.

There are three steps involved:

1 Team members individually write down their own ideas on cards.
2 All the cards are placed on the table or stuck on the wall. Team members then take someone else's card from the table and add to it. A set time is allowed to do this. Members may contribute ideas to as many cards as they wish.
3 Repeat step 2.

Benefits

If there is conflict within the group, or if the subject is likely to be controversial, brainwriting may be more successful than brainstorming. Brainwriting encourages groupwork and consensual teamwork by asking team members to build upon the ideas of others as well as generate ideas of their own. In a situation where it is important to have more developed ideas, brainwriting will prove more useful than brainstorming.

Example

An organization was considering the introduction of flexitime against some known opposition. They decided to use brainwriting in teams to allow everyone to contribute and build a plan for its introduction. They focused on the question 'How do we introduce flexitime successfully?' Everyone used cards to write their own ideas and then contributed by adding to the ideas of others. By focusing on the positive, and generating a depth of ideas, they were able to build a plan for the introduction of flexitime. Team members took responsibility for the ideas that they had originated and helped to bring about a successful outcome.

Reference

Lance Gibbs (1987) 'Tools for problem solving'. London: PA Consulting Group (internal report).

Method 53   Breaking set

Purpose

To overcome blocks in thinking by generating new ideas. It is particularly useful in prompting a group to be more receptive to new suggestions.

When to use

If a group has run out of ideas or has become set on a particular line of thinking.

How to use

The idea, solution or problem is written on a flip chart and is examined by the group, asking several key questions under the following headings:

1 *Adapt*   What else is like this? Are there any parallels in the past? What could we copy? What other ideas are like this?
2 *Modify*   Can we change the meaning, colour, sound, smell, feel, form, shape?
3 *Magnify*   What can be added? More time, height, size? Duplicate, multiply, exaggerate?
4 *Minimize*   What can be taken away? Smaller, condensed, simplified, streamlined, split up, omitted?
5 *Substitute*   Who else, what else, instead? Other suppliers, components, materials, power, processes, approaches?
6 *Rearrange*   Swap cause and effect? Other pattern, layout, sequence, schedule?
7 *Reverse*   What are the opposites? Swap positive and negative? Turn it round, upside down, change roles?
8 *Combine*   Combine purposes, elements, ideas, blend, assortment, ensemble?

Benefits

Different ways of viewing the same idea are a good means of generating more ideas. Often when a group has tried something and failed, it is reluctant to change track. Breaking set provides a way of building on an existing idea to generate new ideas.

Example

An organization was looking for a novel design for a lead grid used in automotive battery manufacture. The grid itself had to conduct electricity, have a certain physical strength and be able to have paste stuck to it. There were no other characteristics. The grid had been made of gravity cast lead in the past.

Adapt   Net curtains, the front of an old wireless.
Modify   Cylindrical, round, hexagonal.
Magnify   Continuous not discrete grids.
Minimize   More holes, less metal, thinner.
Substitute Spines not a grid.
Rearrange   Change the horizontal and vertical axes.
Reverse   Stack the grids rather than hanging as before.

The design changed as a result to an expanded grid (net curtains) that was continuously cast rather than gravity cast.

Method 54   Buzz groups

Purpose

A way of getting the immediate reaction of a group to a new idea or problem.

When to use

Buzz groups are used to generate energy when a group is stagnating. They are very useful for changing the focus from previous work and bringing everyone back into the discussion.

How to use

Buzz groups work best for small numbers of people. A maximum size of four is suggested.

Ask the group members to form several small groups and ask them a simple question or allocate a simple task. The question could be 'What do you want to do now?', 'Where shall we eat tonight?' or 'How shall we recognize successful project teams?' The task could be 'allocate the workshop into teams of two for the next session'. They are asked to report back on their discussions.

Benefits

The benefit comes in changing tack and generating lively discussion. Buzz groups are very noisy and bring people back into the workshop. They can also be useful if, as workshop leader, you need to refocus the direction of the workshop.

Example

A company implementing the TQM process used the buzz groups technique at the beginning of each training session to record current problems and get people in the right frame of mind for the training to come.

Reference
T. Bourner, V. Martin and P. Race (1993) *Workshops that Work*. New York: McGraw-Hill.

Method 55   Idea writing

Purpose

To bring all participants into groupwork.

When to use

Idea writing is used to generate energy when a group is stagnating. It is useful for changing the focus from previous work and bringing everyone back into the discussion.

How to use

Idea writing is a very simple process involving five steps:

1   Break the workshop participants into subgroups of about four or five people and give everyone an idea writing sheet.

```
┌─────────────────────────────────────────┐
│             IDEA WRITING SHEET            │
├─────────────────────────────────────────┤
│  Name ..................................  │
│  My question or statement                 │
├─────────────────────────────────────────┤
│                                           │
│                                           │
├─────────────────────────────────────────┤
│  First response                           │
├─────────────────────────────────────────┤
│                                           │
│                                           │
├─────────────────────────────────────────┤
│  Response of other participants           │
├─────────────────────────────────────────┤
│                                           │
│                                           │
├─────────────────────────────────────────┤
│                                           │
└─────────────────────────────────────────┘
```

Figure 1   *Typical idea writing sheet*

2   Each participant writes his or her name and a statement or question on which comment is invited.
3   He or she then writes his or her own response to the statement or question on the same sheet.
4   The sheets are passed to other members of the subgroup who add their own responses to the sheet. All writing should be completed in a maximum of 30 minutes and should be done silently.
5   When complete, the original writer reads out the question and all the responses to it, using it to generate discussion.

Benefits

The benefit of idea writing is as a diversion when the workshop leader judges that the participants need some quiet time. It is particularly useful in traditional 'low' sessions, such as after lunch, as it involves little energetic activity but much thought.

Example

A typical idea writing sheet is given in Figure 1.

Reference

T. Bourner, V. Martin and P. Race (1993) *Workshops that Work*. New York: McGraw-Hill.

Method 56   Imagineering

Purpose

To assist a company to identify areas of opportunity by concentrating on the ideal outcome then working back from it.

When to use

When clarifying vision and building a list of actions to assist in planning what to do.

How to use

There are five steps in imagineering:

1 Brainstorm a list of features that characterize the ideal situation. This list can be developed in a group atmosphere involving everyone.
2 For each of the preferred or actual characteristics identified, state the actual current situation in relation to it.
3 For each of the characteristics, identify the gap to be bridged to bring about the ideal situation.
4 Use cause and effect analysis to break down the gap into small areas that can then be addressed.
5 For each of the small areas identified, agree an owner and time-scale for completion.

Benefits

Imagineering breaks down what can seem a daunting task into a list of actions which can be individually achieved.

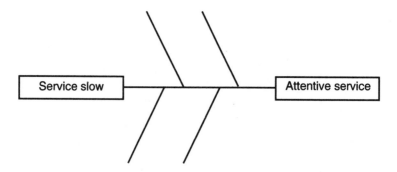

Figure 1   *Imagineering diagram to bridge gap from actual to ideal situation*

Example

The manager of a bank is engaged in a customer care programme and is working out what is the ideal situation for the bank's customers. The first stage is to brainstorm a list of *ideal* characteristics: for example, warm greeting, attentive service, pleasant atmosphere, privacy as desired etc. The next stage is to identify the *actual* current situation: for example, staff unfriendly, service slow, dingy surroundings, open plan only etc. The third stage is to identify the causes and the gap to be filled. For each of the constituent parts (Figure 1) a plan is then drawn up to bridge the gap.

Method 57   Improve internal process (IIP) plan

Purpose

To provide the structure to develop work plan details for a task using various factors, such as measurables, responsible resources, times and previous task owners.

When to use

When you want to improve internal process (IIP) by using information at a specific level of the development of the project or task.

How to use

1   List and number each task.
2   Provide the measure of completion for each task. The measure should be clearly defined data, quantity and level of performance.
3   Allocate responsibility for completion of each task.
4   Give details of the resources required for each task.
5   Write down the time when each task will be completed.
6   Find the previous owner for each task.

Benefits

It provides the structure to improve internal process.

Example

An example of the information matrix required for an IIP plan is given below in Figure 1.

No.	Task	Allocation	Overall responsibility	Measurement	Resources	Time	Previous owner
1	Meet the deadline						
2	Status of each order						
3	Meeting delivery date						
4	Sending the correct order						
5	Packaged properly	Mike A.	Gopal K.	Zero defect	Packaging material	6 weeks	Mike A.

Figure 1   *Information matrix required for IIP*

Method 58   Lateral thinking

Purpose

A way of transferring from one frame of reference to another, enabling you to break down barriers which inhibit creative thought.

When to use

Lateral thinking is used when a team is trying to identify problems or possible solutions. It can also be used as a diversion to relax a workshop group.

How to use

There are several well-established ways of beginning lateral thinking.

Mixing metaphors

This involves using a metaphor to bring a new look to a situation or problem. Suppose that you are planning to introduce statistical process control and are experiencing problems of acceptance at middle management level. Think of something that has parallels with introducing a change; for example, redecorating a room. Now imagine what you can do to make the redecoration as successful as possible. Brainstorm a list of ideas.

Now, for each idea, discuss how it relates to the introduction of statistical process control (SPC). An example might be 'make it more light'. The parallel with SPC might be to look at education and training and consider attitudes.

Random juxtaposition

This involves introducing a completely new notion to allow more ideas to be generated.

A group may be considering factors in the design of school rooms. At a certain stage, the idea of 'infants' might be introduced to extend the scope of the ideas generated.

Stopping no

This involves what de Bono (1970) calls the 'intermediate impossible'. The idea is best illustrated by an example. An organization is experiencing problems with the outgoing quality of product. The first response is 'We can't afford to employ any more inspectors.' The 'intermediate impossible' would be 'Make everyone an inspector.' This would result in changes in role and training to allow everyone to take responsibility for their own work.

Benefits

Established patterns of thought can stand in the way of innovative ideas. Lateral thinking provides a way of removing barriers to new ideas.

Example

Lateral thinking was used by an organization looking for different ways of marketing a five-day residential course. Random juxtaposition was used and the idea 'spouses' was introduced. As a result, the organization offered a deal for spouses that included a day at the races following the course.

Reference

Edward de Bono (1970) *Lateral Thinking*. New York: Harper and Row.

Method 59   List reduction

Purpose

To reduce a list of ideas to one of manageable size.

When to use

At the end of a brainstorming session or any session involving the generation of ideas.

How to use

There are two main ways of reducing lists of ideas. These are 'hurdling' and 'voting'.

Hurdling

A way of testing the items on the list against a list of hurdles or criteria. Examples of this might be 'Achievable in 8 weeks' or 'Costs less than £10,000'. Those items that fail to jump the hurdle are then discarded.

This idea can be extended by compiling a list of 'musts' and 'wants'. The list is divided into the two categories. If there are no 'wants', this can be achieved by weighting the 'musts' by giving each a score on a scale 1–5. The higher the score the more important the 'must'. Again, only those items that clear the hurdles remain on the list.

Voting

It can be used by itself or with hurdling. The team decides how many votes each person can be allocated. Each team member then allocates their votes among the ideas generated. The ideas receiving fewest votes are crossed off and the process is repeated until a final list of the key ideas is reached.

Benefits

Dealing with a very long list of ideas generated during a brainstorm can be daunting. List reduction gives a structured approach to this task.

Example

A brainstorming session examined ways of reducing sickness absence. At the end of the session, the group used hurdles to reduce the list generated. The hurdles used were, first, 'Will not lead directly to industrial unrest' and, secondly, 'Can be introduced at no additional cost.' The reduced list formed the basis of an action plan.

Reference

T. Bourner, V. Martin and P. Race (1993) *Workshops that Work*. New York: McGraw-Hill.

Method 60   Mind mapping

Purpose

A way of generating and recording ideas individually rather than in a group. Mind mapping makes use of word associations, encouraging you to follow your own thought patterns, wherever they may lead. It also provides a written record of the ideas generated.

When to use

It can be used as an alternative to list-making as a way of generating ideas.

How to use

There are six simple steps involved:

1 Place the topic, issue or problem at the centre of a large clean sheet of paper.
2 Allow your mind to wander about the topic.
3 Starting with your first thought, draw a line from the centre and label it, writing along the line. Follow the thought by drawing branches out from the line, labelling them as you go.
4 Without pausing, when one idea runs out, start a new one with a new line starting from the centre.
5 Take care not to evaluate or criticize what you have written down. Write down all ideas as they occur.
6 When the ideas dry up, take a different coloured pen and join up ideas associated with each other.

Benefits

Often when you are thinking creatively about a problem, part of the thought flow gets lost and it is difficult to recreate it. The output formed by mind mapping provides an excellent reminder of your train of thought.

Example

An example of mind mapping is shown in Figure 1.

Reference

Tony Buzan (1974) *Use your Head*. London: Ariel Books.

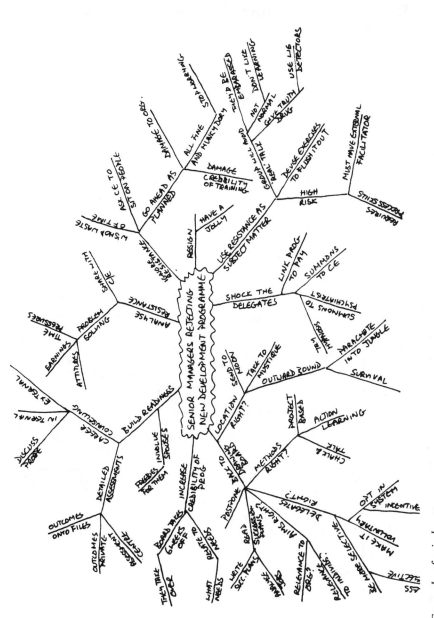

Figure 1 *Example of mind map*

Method 61   Morphological forced connections

Purpose

To generate new ideas or ways of approaching problems. It combines lists of attributes and forces new connections between them, so triggering new options.

When to use

To find new ways of approaching an old problem when old assumptions about the problem are blocking perception about what can be done.

How to use

There are four simple steps:

Attributes	Advertising	Target	Costs	Location	Timing
Current methods	QA News	QA Mgrs	200/day	Home counties	1/2 days
Alternative methods	Libraries	Unemployed	£30	Abroad	2 hrs
	Works Mgt	Executives	£85	Schools	Sunday
	TECs	MBAs		Open learning	Weekends
	Chambers of Commerce	School leavers			After work
	Betting shops				Between shifts
	Direct mail				
	Prisons				

Figure 1   *Morphological forced connections*

1 List in a row along the top of a flip chart the main attributes or characteristics of the approach or device currently used.
2 Below each attribute, list as many alternatives as possible without any evaluation or censorship.
3 Generate several different 'forced connections' across the columns. Join them up.
4 Follow through by generating new ideas, or by agreeing to examine any likely ideas found.

Benefits

When it is difficult to think of new ways to approach an old topic, forced connections generate possible new approaches that allow you to break form out-of-date assumptions.

Example

The example in Figure 1 shows forced connections used to generate alternative ways of marketing quality management courses. The ideas joined together form a new idea for marketing the courses. The organization decided to advertise in the TECs aiming at the unemployed and run the courses in schools at weekends.

Method 62   Multi-voting

Purpose

To select the most popular or important items from a list.

When to use

Multi-voting is often used at the end of a brainstorming session when trying to reduce the list of items to a more manageable size.

How to use

Multi-voting is conducted by using a series of votes, each cutting the list in half, allowing the fast reduction of large lists of ideas.

1 Generate a list of items; for example, ideas by brainstorming.
2 Combine any similar items.
3 Number the items.
4 Each team member is allocated a number of votes equal to one-third of the total number of items on the list. They allocate these votes to the number of the item. Only one vote per item per team member is allowed.
5 The team members then call out their votes as each item number in turn is discussed.
6 Eliminate those with one vote or less. If the team is large, this number may be increased to two or three.
7 Renumber the list and repeat steps 4–6 until only a few items remain. If at this stage there is no clear favourite, use paired comparisons to reach a final conclusion.

Benefits

Multi-voting aids the reduction of a large list of items.

Example

At the end of a workshop which had developed a list of critical business processes, the group used multi-voting to reduce the initial catalogue of 78 processes to a manageable list of seven.

Reference

Arturo Onnies (1992) *The Language of Total Quality*. Castellamonte: T PoK Publication on Quality, Italy.

Method 63 Nominal group technique

Purpose

A way of generating ideas from a group and identifying the level of support within the group for those ideas.

When to use

When a group is trying to reach a conclusion on a collective course of action or when one individual is dominating a group and you want to involve others. It can also be used at the end of a brainstorming session to bring together the ideas.

How to use

This is a very simple technique that involves six steps:

1 Agree a group leader to record the ideas on a flip chart.
2 The leader asks each group member in turn to give an idea or suggestion and records this on the flip chart. There is no discussion or evaluation of the ideas at this stage. As with brainstorming, the ideas should be there for all to see.
3 Repeat step 2 until all the ideas that the group has have been exhausted.
4 Allow the group members to seek clarification of any suggestions that they do not understand.
5 Ask each group member to write down on a piece of paper their five most important ideas in order, giving the score of 5 to the most important, down to 1 for the least important. When this is complete, the members are asked to record their scores on the flip chart next to the idea being evaluated.
6 The group leader adds up all the scores and reports the results. If the group began with a lot of ideas it may be necessary to go through the process twice to reach a conclusion.

Benefits

To add structure and therefore control to an idea-generating session. The group leaves the session committed to the outcome. It can also be useful for a workshop leader needing to exert control and bring a group back to order.

The technique can be varied, for example, by giving group members coloured markers and using these to do the final scoring, or by simply giving five votes and allocating these between ideas.

Example

Nominal group technique was used at the end of a workshop where the leader was having difficulty bringing the session to a close. The technique was used to generate and agree a list of critical barriers to the implementation of total quality. The approach was especially useful as the atmosphere was emotionally charged and the leader needed to calm the situation.

Reference

T. Bourner, V. Martin and P. Race (1993) *Workshops that Work*. New York: McGraw-Hill.

Method 64   Opportunity analysis

Purpose

Offers the opportunity to evaluate quickly a long list of options against desired goals and available resources.

When to use

This method can be used by an individual or group when presented with many opportunities where it is difficult to decide what to do first.

How to use

1 Write down all your goals in the situation under review.
2 Rank the importance (to satisfy the customer) of each goal, and rate your ability to complete them.
3 Do you have the required resources?

Benefits

It provides a rapid evaluation of a long list of options in relation to desired goals and the available resources.

Goals	Importance High Medium Low			Ability to complete High Medium Low		
1 Provide timely invoice	X					X
2 Match delivery date as requested	X			X		
3 Update all the information regularly		X				X
4 Send goods to the order	X			X		
5 Send complete order		X			X	
6 Pack products properly		X		X		

Figure 1   *Opportunity analysis*

Example

Figure 1 provides an opportunity analysis for a company that wants to satisfy its customer requirements. Here items 2 and 4 of 'High importance' and 'High ability to complete' should be done first.

Method 65   Rich pictures

Purpose

To allow a group to capture all ideas developed, without judgement or analysis, in a pictorial form that allows the strength of the ideas to be recorded.

When to use

When a group is examining a problem, a rich picture can be developed to show what areas the group has considered so that all thoughts about the problem are taken into account.

How to use

A rich picture develops a line of thought as it occurs without reaching conclusions.

Benefits

During teamwork, the strength of an idea, or the way that it is expressed, often tempts the group into coming to conclusions too early in the process. Rich pictures capture those ideas and allow the team to move on. The pictures form a more evocative record of the groupwork and make it far easier to remember the discussion than is the case with written records.

Example

In Figure 1, a team has been examining quality of service issues in a hotel chain. The picture shows the data as they were collected without analysis or judgement. Following the team meeting, the ideas where taken off the rich picture and turned into a plan of action.

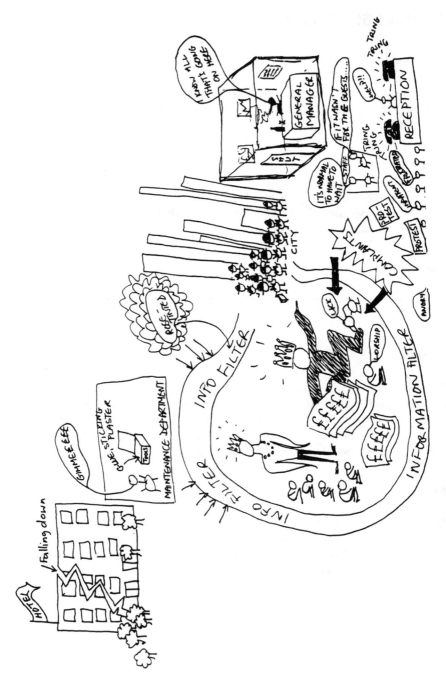

Figure 1   *Rich pictures generated during groupwork on hotel service issues*

Method 66   Snowballing

Purpose

Sometimes called 'pyramiding', snowballing is a technique for gathering information or ideas.

When to use

In a workshop setting, where participants do not know each other, snowballing is an excellent way of breaking the ice and helping members get to know each other.

How to use

This is a very easy technique for idea generation. There are four simple stages:

1   Participants are given a task which is to be carried out individually. The task should involve writing down ideas or information on paper.
2   Participants are then paired together and asked to continue the task, taking it further.
3   The pairs are then made into groups of four and asked to continue the task.
4   The combining is continued until all the workshop participants are involved in one group.

Benefits

Snowballing allows everyone with ideas to contribute to the work of the group without the embarrassment of having to speak individually. It also allows ownership of ideas to develop in the group.

An additional use of snowballing is when a group is becoming rowdy and the group leader is seeking to re-exert control. The technique breaks the group away from what it was doing and gives the participants a specific task, quietening them down.

Example

A workshop group of eight directors is considering what key performance indicators to set for their business:

Stage 1   Individually write down their ideas about the indicators.
Stage 2   In pairs combine their lists and reduce the number of indicators to 5.
Stage 3   In groups of four combine the lists and again reduce the number of indicators to 5.
Stage 4   As a whole group debate the two lists, combine them and reduce the final number of indicators.

Reference

T. Bourner, V. Martin and P. Race (1993) *Workshops that Work*. New York: McGraw-Hill.

Method 67   Suggestion schemes

Purpose

To generate ideas for improvement.

When to use

At a later stage of a total quality process when there is a quality improvement plan in place and a mechanism for selecting ideas for action.

How to use

Suggestion schemes can seem deceptively simple and many fail because ideas are asked for without any mechanism being set up for decision-taking or communication of those decisions. The following are guidelines for running successful suggestion schemes:

1   Set up a steering group to oversee the process.
2   Delegate as far down as practical the decision on whether or not to implement the suggestion.
3   Give awards to supervisors and managers whose employees generate most ideas.
4   In the early stages go for quantity of ideas rather than quality.
5   To generate ideas in manageable numbers try to set themes for ideas and change the themes regularly.
6   Ensure that all ideas are acknowledged quickly and that the person generating the idea is told whether it is to be implemented and, if not, why not.
7   Look for reasons to say 'yes' rather than 'no'.
8   In the early stages be prepared for ideas to be about environmental aspects rather than operational ones.

Benefits

Suggestion schemes provide a way of moving to continuous improvement via small incremental changes.

Example

A head office function of a major service organization introduced a suggestion scheme as part of its total quality process. In the first year 18 suggestions per employee were generated and 90 per cent acted upon. The organization began a 'Suggestion of the month' and 'Suggestion of the year' award and the scheme flourished.

DATA COLLECTION, ANALYSIS AND DISPLAY

Method 68   Bar charts

Purpose

To display discrete data collected by checksheets so that patterns can be discovered.

When to use

In the early stages of problem-solving when a team is trying to find out what is happening.

How to use

The number of times an event occurs is shown on the vertical axis. The value at which it occurs is shown on the horizontal axis. Figure 1 shows a bar chart of the reasons for in-test failure of a printed circuit board. Bar charts are sometimes used in conjunction with *Pareto analysis* (Method 20).

Benefits

Bar charts give a simple pictorial representation of data.

Example

The following data were used to produce the bar chart in Figure 1:

Failure code	Explanation	No. failing
A	Missing component	1,187
B	Wrong component	980
C	Wrongly inserted	767
D	Cold solder joint	420
E	Short pins	409
F	Test machine fault	221

The bar chart shows clearly which reasons for failure need to be addressed to have any impact on the problem.

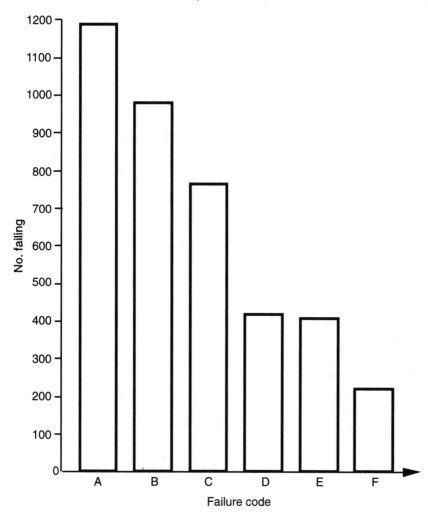

Figure 1   *Bar chart of printed circuit board*

Reference

H. Kume (1985) *Statistical Methods for Quality Improvement*. Tokyo: AOTS.

Method 69   Basic statistics

Purpose

The mean, median, mode, range and standard deviation are ways of summarizing and describing large volumes of data. The first three are measures of location; the last two are measures of spread.

When to use

When looking for patterns in data or when trying to compare large volumes of data, these parameters give statistically based measures that aid decision-taking.

How to use

The mean

The mean is the simple arithmetic average of all the data points. To calculate the mean, add together all the points and divide by the number of points in the sum.

The mean is usually written $\bar{X}$ (pronounced X bar). The formula is

$$\bar{X} = \frac{\Sigma(x_1 + x_2 + x_3 + \ldots \ldots .x_n)}{n}$$

where there are n points called x_1 to x_n.

As an example, the following list gives the voltage derived from a circuit having variability due to poor tolerance control:

1.1	1.2	1.2	1.3
1.3	1.3	1.4	1.4
1.4	1.4	1.5	1.5
1.5	1.6	1.6	1.6
1.7	1.7	1.7	1.8
1.8	1.8	1.9	1.9
1.9	1.9	1.9	2.0
2.0	2.0	2.0	2.1
2.1	2.1	2.2	2.2
2.3			

There are 37 points in total.

The sum ΣX is $1.1 + 1.2 + \ldots + 2.3 = 63.3$.
The mean voltage $\bar{X} = 63.3/37 = 1.71$.

The median

The median is the 50 per cent point, the point above which and below which half of the points lie. There is no formula for calculating the median. As an example, the above data are laid out in the form of a tally chart as follows:

Value	Count	Cumulative count
1.1	1	1
1.2	2	3
1.3	3	6
1.4	4	10
1.5	3	13
1.6	3	16
1.7	3	19
1.8	3	22
1.9	5	27
2.0	4	31
2.1	3	34
2.2	2	36
2.3	1	37

The median will be the 19th point, somewhere between 1.7 and 1.8. It could be described as 1.7+ volts.

The mode

This is simply the most frequently occurring point. For example, in the data above, it is 1.9 volts. When the data are symmetrical about the mean, the mean, median and mode have the same value.

The range

The range is a measure of the overall spread of a set of values. It is defined as the arithmetic difference between the largest and smallest value. In the above example, the largest value is 2.3 and the smallest value is 1.1 so the range is $2.3 - 1.1 = 1.2$ volts.

The standard deviation

The standard deviation is otherwise known as the root mean square deviation of all values from the mean. It is calculated by taking the difference of each value away from the mean, squaring it, and adding it to all the other squared deviations. The total is then divided by the number of values involved minus 1. The square root is then taken. This is written:

$$\sqrt{\frac{(X_i - \bar{X})^2}{n - 1}}$$

In the example the calculation is:

$$\frac{(1.1 - 1.71)^2 + (1.2 - 1.71)^2 + \ldots + (2.3 - 1.71)^2}{36}$$

$$= \sqrt{\frac{3.7757}{36}} = \sqrt{0.10488} = 0.32 \text{ volts.}$$

There are simple methods of testing whether means, ranges and standard deviations of different samples differ statistically.

Benefits

Statistical techniques use the basic data and provide facts upon which decisions can be made.

Example

Examples of the mean, median, mode, range and standard deviation are given above.

Reference

G.K. Kanji (1993) *100 Statistical Tests*. London: Sage.

Method 70   Box and whisker plots

Purpose

To provide a simple way of drawing the basic shape of the distribution of a set of data.

When to use

In quality monitoring presentation when you want to describe the distribution of large data and their dispersion in order to carry out exploratory data analysis.

How to use

The central box contains the central half of the data with the end of the box marking the quartiles and the central line the median. The whiskers go out to the extreme values.

   With larger data sets, there is a convention that the whisker lines enclose, say, 97.5 per cent of the data with more extreme values marked individually. With small data sets, the whiskers end at the largest and smallest values.

Benefits

Sample method to describe the distribution of data and their variability. In particular, they help to explore large data in the work of process control.

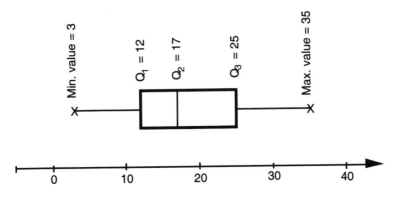

Figure 1   *A box and whisker plot*

Example

A box and whisker plot for data containing 50 observations is given in Figure 1.

7	10	32	17	21	29	13	3	18	28
18	6	12	14	25	27	33	29	17	12
8	35	16	31	11	15	22	7	20	9
19	19	5	21	8	13	17	30	14	15
33	18	7	11	13	25	15	16	23	28

Here, Q_1 = 1st quartile   (25%) Min. value = 3
Q_2 = Median   (50%) Max. value = 30
Q_3 = 3rd quartile   (75%)

References

B. Bergman and B. Klefsjo (1994) *Quality: from Customer Needs to Customer Satisfaction.* New York: McGraw-Hill.

J. Tukey (1991) *Exploratory Data Analysis.* New York: Addison-Wesley.

Method 71   *C* chart

Purpose

To identify when the number of defects in a sample of constant size is changing over time.

When to use

When monitoring a process to detect changes or, when a change has been made to process inputs, to find out whether the number of defects or problems also changes. *C* charts are used when the sample size is constant, or does not vary by more than 25 per cent of the average sample size.

How to use

There are six simple steps involved:

1 Collect data showing the number of problems or defects over time. Draw up a table showing the number of defects for each lot number. The number of defects is called *C*. The total number of lots is called *m*.
2 Plot the data from the table onto the *C* control chart. The successive lot numbers are shown on the horizontal axis, the number of defects or problems *C* is shown on the vertical axis.
3 Calculate the centre line $\bar{C}$. This is calculated as the sum of all the *C*s divided by the sum of all the *n*s and is written as:

$$\bar{C} = \Sigma C / \Sigma n$$

4 Calculate the control limits which are ± 3 s.d. about the central line. They are calculated as

$$\text{Upper control limit (UCL)} = \bar{C} + 3\sqrt{\bar{C}}$$
$$\text{Lower control limit (LCL)} = \bar{C} - 3\sqrt{\bar{C}}$$

If the lower control limit is less than zero it is taken to be zero.
5 Draw the central line and the control limits on the control chart.
6 Interpret the results.

Benefits

It can be difficult to separate out random variation (often called common cause or non-assignable variation) from real variation caused by changes to the process. C charts give a way to do this for the number of defects or problems with a sample size that is constant.

Example

An organization is experiencing problems with the number of errors or mis-codings of invoices and a C chart was used to monitor the error rate. A constant number of 80 invoices was sampled each week with the following results (see Figure 1).

Lot no.	No. of errors
1	5
2	3
3	0
4	4
5	7
6	0
7	2
8	9
9	5
10	6
11	0
12	8
13	5
14	0
15	6
16	2
17	7
18	0
19	7
20	4

For the data above the calculations were as follows:

$$n = 80 \; m = 20$$
$$\text{CL} = \bar{C} = \frac{\Sigma C}{m} = \frac{80}{20} = 4$$
$$K = 3\sqrt{\bar{C}} = 3\sqrt{4} = 6$$
$$\text{UCL} = \bar{C} + K = 10$$
$$\text{LCL} = \bar{C} - K = 0$$

Reference

D.M. Amsden, H.E. Butler and R.T. Amsden (1991) *SPC Simplified for Services*. London: Chapman and Hall.

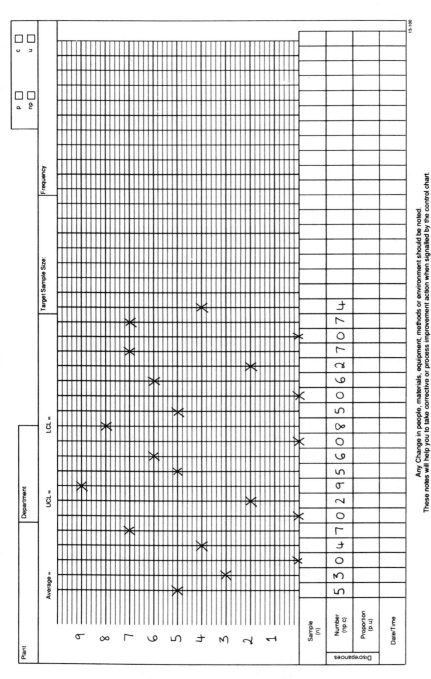

Figure 1 *Bar chart of printed circuit board*

Method 72   Checksheets

Purpose

To collect data when the number of times a defect or value occurs is important.

When to use

Either during problem definition when you are collecting data to find out what is happening, or when you have implemented a solution and you are collecting data to monitor the new situation.

How to use

There are five simple steps to draw a checksheet diagram:

1   Agree the data to be collected. This step is vital: you cannot analyse data that have not been collected.
2   Design the checksheet.
3   Test the checksheet using someone who has not been involved in the design. Get him or her to use the checksheet without assistance. If necessary, modify the checksheet.
4   Design a master checksheet. If more than one person is to be involved in data collection, you will need to bring together all the data collected. The way to do this is to use a master checksheet.
5   Collect the data.

Day	Absences	Total
Monday	𝓗𝓣𝓣 𝓙𝓗𝓣 𝕀𝓛𝓧 𝓙𝓗𝓧 𝕀𝕀	22
Tuesday	𝓙𝓗𝓣 𝕀	6
Wednesday	𝕀𝕀𝕀	3
Thursday	𝕀∕𝕀𝕀	4
Friday	𝓗𝓣𝓣 𝓙𝓗𝓣 𝓙𝓗𝓣 𝕀∕𝕀	18

Figure 1   *Checksheet on absenteeism*

Benefits

By establishing the facts about the incidence of failure, a team can plan to identify the causes of failure and look for ways of removing them. Actions are taken on the basis of evidence, not feeling.

Checksheets are an excellent way of involving people in quality improvement. They give a simple method of data collection that can be easily understood and applied in a wide range of areas.

Example

During an attempt to reduce unauthorized absence from work, a team collected data on the day of the week that absences occurred. The checksheet shown in Figure 1 gives the results of the study over a six-month period. The team used the data in consultation with departmental managers to crack down on absenteeism.

Reference

H. Kume (1985) *Statistical Methods for Quality Improvement*. Tokyo: AOTS.

Method 73   Concentration diagrams

Purpose

To collect data when the location of a defect or problem is important.

When to use

Either during problem definition when you are collecting data to find out what is happening, or when you have implemented a solution and you are collecting data to monitor the new situation.

How to use

There are five simple steps to draw a concentration diagram:

1   Agree the data to be collected. This step is vital: you cannot analyse data that have not been collected.
2   Design the concentration diagram.
3   Test the diagram using someone who has not been involved in the design. Get him or her to use the diagram without assistance. If necessary, modify the diagram.
4   Design a master concentration diagram. If more than one person is to be involved in data collection, you will need to bring together all the data collected. The way to do this is to use a master diagram.
5   Collect the data.

Benefits

By establishing the facts about the location of failure, a team can plan to identify the causes of failure and look for ways of removing them. Actions are taken on the basis of evidence, not feeling.

Concentration diagrams are an excellent way of involving people in administration areas in quality improvement. They provide a simple method of data collection that can be easily understood and applied in office areas.

Example

A large organization was concerned about the number of road accidents happening on the site, covering approximately 10 miles by 3 miles.

In an attempt to find out why the accidents were happening, the road map of the site was used as a concentration diagram and each time an accident occurred the position of the accident was recorded on the map. The concentration diagram showed clear patterns in the location of accidents.

The organization used the information to place 'sleeping policemen' and traffic lights to slow down the traffic at the places where most accidents had been happening. The situation was monitored and a fall in the number of accidents was noted.

Method 74   Cusum chart

Purpose

To identify when the mean value is changing over time.

When to use

When monitoring a process to detect changes, or when a change has been made to process inputs to find out whether the mean changes. Cumulative sum (or cusum) charts can be used to monitor both variables and attributes data, and are particularly useful for detecting long-term trends in data.

How to use

There are six simple steps involved:

1   Collect the data. Cusums are particularly useful for plotting daily or weekly averages.
2   Decide which value to subtract from each value. The values used most often are the overall mean and the target value. Cusums are very sensitive to the value selected. Too large a value and the cusum will disappear off the bottom of the chart; too small a value and it disappears off the top. If in doubt, the overall mean should be used, in this case the cusum will end on the x axis.
3   Subtract this value from each data element. The resulting number is called the residual.
4   Accumulate the residual values.
5   Plot the accumulated residuals on the y axis and the time on the x axis.
6   Interpret the results. A change in mean value is shown by a change in slope. If the cusum is moving downwards, the current mean is less than average; if it is moving upwards, more than average.

Benefits

Cusum charts are very sensitive to change and so can give very fast warning of process changes. They are also very accurate so can often pinpoint exactly when a change occurred. The downside of these two characteristics is that they can sometimes detect unreal changes.

Cusums can also be used as part of experimental design when trying to relate input and output variables. Concurrent changes in both charts

Table 1 *Cusum data and values*

Week no.	Productivity value (%)	Cusum value	
		$X-T$	$\Sigma(X-T)$
1	57	−5	−5
2	69	7	2
3	64	2	4
4	54	−8	−4
5	52	−10	−14
6	76	14	0
7	71	9	9
8	51	−11	−2
9	53	−9	−11
10	69	7	−4
11	71	9	5
12	61	−1	4
13	55	−7	−3
14	80	18	15
15	81	19	34
16	64	2	36
17	71	9	45
18	58	−4	41
19	63	1	42
20	76	14	56
21	95	33	89
22	65	3	92

suggest that there is a linkage and that the input variable is affecting the output. This then needs to be checked statistically.

Example

An insurance company was planning to carry out some training in the claims handling department, aimed at improving productivity. The company decided to use a cusum to monitor individual productivity to assess how effective the training was. The target value chosen from historic data for each worker's productivity was 62 per cent. The data collected and cusum values are given in Table 1.

The cusum chart (Figure 1) clearly shows a change following week 13 when the training course took place. From week 1 to week 13 the productivity value was approximately 62 per cent, the historic value. From week 13, the slope of the cusum changed, corresponding to a new value of 74 per cent. The training course had been effective.

Reference

M. Owen (1989a) *SPC and Business Improvement*. London: IFS Publications.

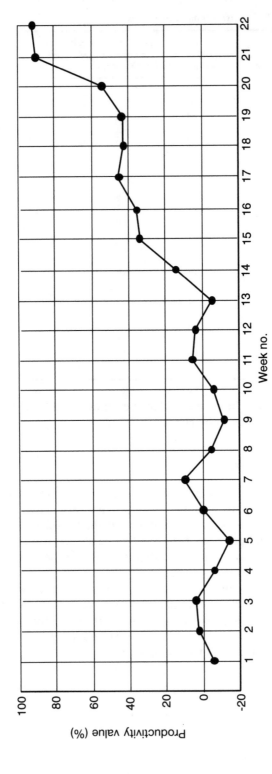

Figure 1   *Cusum chart*

Method 75   Dot plots

Purpose

A simple graphic device which presents observations as dots on a horizontal scale.

When to use

When there are less than 30 observations and you want to use a simple diagram on a piece of paper without any fuss.

How to use

Draw a horizontal scale and mark the observation above it with dots.

Benefits

Very easy to use and useful when you have fewer than 30 observations. It is also useful when you are comparing two samples.

Figure 1   *Dot plot*

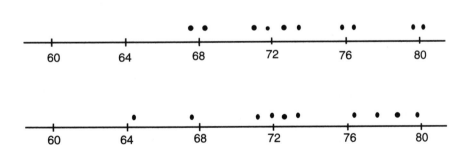

Figure 2   *Dot plot for two samples*

Example

Figure 1 shows a dot plot of a process yield of ten runs in a chemical plant.

66 77 68 69 71 70 72 73 62 75   (sample)

Figure 2 shows the composition of two samples of a process yield from a chemical plant by dot plots.

Sample 1: 72 71 73 76 74 77 69 80 68 79
Sample 2: 72 74 79 73 71 67 78 77 80 65

Here we see that the averages of the two samples are about the same, but sample 1 has less variation than sample 2.

Reference

P.W.M. John (1990) *Statistical Methods in Engineering and Quality Assurance*. New York: Wiley.

Method 76   Flowcharts

Purpose

To generate a picture of how work gets done by linking together all the steps taken in a process.

When to use

When a team is working on process improvement, it is first necessary for all members of the team to have a common understanding of the process.

Flowcharts are also a necessary stage in the introduction of ISO 9000.

How to use

Having the correct team is essential when drawing a flowchart. It is necessary to involve all those who are concerned with the process.

There is a simple procedure to follow when drawing a flowchart:

1   Brainstorm all the individual activities that make up the process.
2   List the activities in the order in which they are done.
3   Using wallpaper or some other large sheets of paper, draw out the activities in schematic form. Common flowcharting symbols are shown in Figure 1.
4   Ask each member of the group in turn whether any activities have been missed out and whether he or she agrees with the process as drawn. Make changes as necessary.
5   Test the flowchart by taking an example and 'walking it through' the flowchart.

Benefits

Often processes in organizations are not designed, but have evolved over time. Flowcharting allows processes to be challenged, and gaps, duplications and dead ends identified. It therefore leads to process simplification.

Example

Figure 1 gives a flowchart for drawing a flowchart.

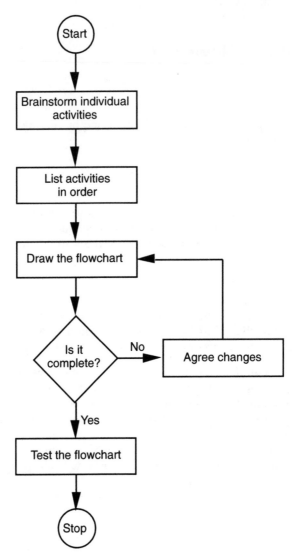

Figure 1   *Flowchart for drawing a flowchart*

Reference

Gary Born (1994) *Process Management to Quality Improvement.* New York: Wiley.

Method 77   Geometric moving average

Purpose

To identify trends in small changes in the process mean. The geometric moving average is sometimes called the exponentially weighted moving average (EWMA).

When to use

When monitoring a process to detect changes in the process mean, or when a change has been made to process inputs to find out whether the process mean changes. Geometric moving average charts can be used to monitor both variables and attributes data and are particularly useful for detecting long-term trends in data. One advantage is that the procedure provides a forecast of where the process mean will be at the next time period.

How to use

There are four simple steps involved:

1 Collect the data. The type of data could be sales figures, factory volumes, error rate or exchange rate.
2 Calculate the subgroup averages by adding together the data in each subgroup and dividing by the subgroup size.
3 Calculate the overall mean of the data by adding together the subgroup averages and dividing by the number of subgroups. This statistic is designated w_t.
4 For each successive subgroup, calculate the statistic w_t as follows:

$$w_t = r \times \bar{X}_t + (1-r) \times w_{t-1}$$

where r is a constant between 0 and 1. The choice is governed by the trade-off between the need to detect an important change without false alarms. Control limits can also be calculated.

Benefits

Geometric moving average charts are relatively insensitive to short-term changes. This means that their main use is when you are trying to mask short-term variation in the process to highlight longer-term variations. The

Table 1 *Difference between sales targets and achievements*

Subgroup no.	Subgroup average	w
1	0.41	0.1025
2	1.11	0.3544
3	−0.04	0.2558
4	−1.04	−0.0682
5	−0.04	−0.0612
6	−0.68	−0.2159
7	−0.85	−0.3744
8	0.81	−0.0783
9	0.62	−0.0963
10	−0.38	−0.0228
11	0.54	0.1179
12	0.18	0.1134
13	0.33	0.1826
14	0.32	0.2170
15	0.44	0.2728
16	0.22	0.2596
17	0.88	0.4147
18	0.16	0.3510
19	0.95	0.5008
20	1.09	0.6481

technique can also be used to predict where the next data point will be, using past data.

Example

Table 1 shows the difference between sales targets and achievements for a sales team. The data are recorded daily, based upon a sample size of five. The subgroup average is based upon these five readings. The value of r chosen was 0.25.

Reference

Thomas P. Ryan (1989) *Statistical Methods for Quality Improvement*. New York: Wiley Interscience.

Method 78   Histograms

Purpose

To display continuous data collected by checksheets so that any patterns can be discovered.

When to use

At the early stages of problem-solving when a team is trying to find out what is happening.

How to use

There are four simple steps involved:

1   Collect the data using a checksheet.
2   Use the vertical axis to display the number of times each value occurs.
3   Use the horizontal axis to display the values.
4   Interpret the histogram.

   Different patterns of histogram suggest that the problem being studied has particular characteristics. Patterns reveal when two or more things are being mixed; for example, different ways of processing claims. They also show when data are being censored; for example, when someone is failing to record certain data items. They can also indicate when there is time-dependence in the data; for example, when something can take a very long time but when it is impossible to take a short time.

Benefits

Assumptions of normality made about data need to be checked before data can be analysed using statistics that depend upon normality. Histograms are a simple visual way of viewing data that highlights non-normal situations. When these are identified, the data can, if necessary, be analysed further. The picture seen can give useful advice to teams trying to establish facts about what is happening.

Examples

Comb-like histogram

The histogram in Figure 1 shows two sets of haemoglobin measurements taken by two nurses using slightly different methods. The readings they obtained appear slightly displaced on the histogram, implying that the differences in the method of taking the readings are resulting in different haemoglobin readings. It was necessary to standardize the method to obtain repeatable readings. Similar examples would occur in mixing inputs from two suppliers, using a scale that is too fine or in reading errors due, for example, to parallax problems.

Cliff-like histogram

The histogram in Figure 2 shows data where a 'go–no go' gauge prevents the presence of data beyond certain bounds. It would therefore be physically impossible to have a reading below 2.3 mm and this shows as a cliff-like face on the left of the histogram. This occurs where there is censorship of data, where it is physically impossible to produce certain values because of a constraint.

Skew histograms

The histogram in Figure 3 shows data where a mould is exhibiting wear over the period of the shift: the reading is slowly moving to the right. Other examples of this would be age to failure of components or the amount of time to process an insurance claim.

Reference

H. Kume (1985) *Statistical Methods for Quality Improvement*. Tokyo: AOTS.

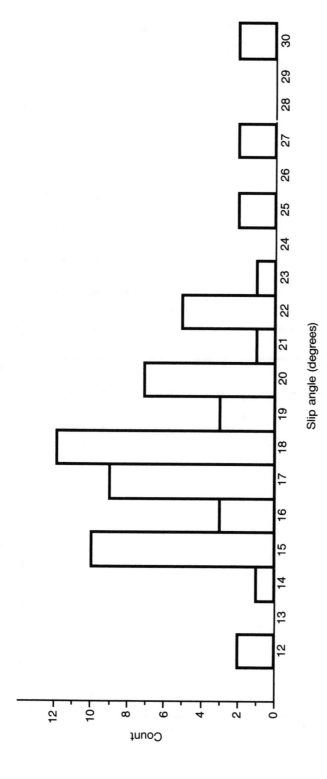

Figure 1 *Comb-like histogram*

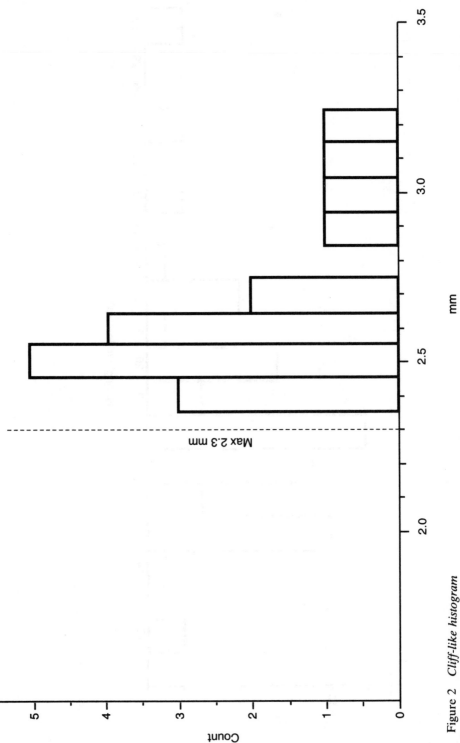

Figure 2   *Cliff-like histogram*

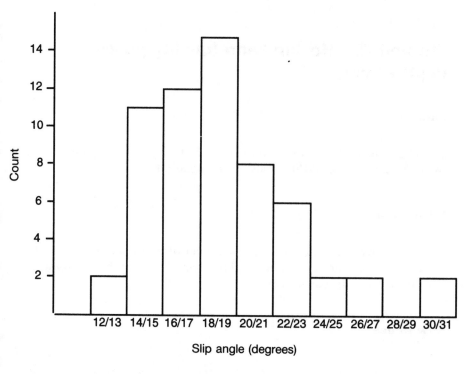

Figure 3 *Skew histogram*

Method 79   Hoshin kanri (quality policy deployment)

Purpose

To delight the customer through the manufacturing and servicing process by implementing the quality goals of the organization.

When to use

When objectives are identified at each level of an organization by top-down and bottom-up consultation and the overall goals of the organization have been set as specific targets.

How to use

1   Define short-term and long-term goals of the organization.
2   Identify the measurable goals.
3   Decide the critical processes involved in achieving these.
4   Ask the teams to agree on performance indicators at appropriate stages of the process.
5   Challenge every level of the process in order to force the organization to change the quality culture.
6   Organizational goals are to be used as measurable goals in order to make the employee understand the importance of the quality improvement process.

Benefits

It shows the employee what the overall goals of the organization are and where he or she fits in so that everybody pulls in the same direction towards clearly defined goals.

Example

Examples of goals set at different levels of an organization, making them evident in all organization processes, are as follows:

Level	Goal
Corporate	Delight the customer
Department	Reduce cost of poor quality
Maintenance	Reduce machine failure by 20 per cent
Manufacturing	Less than 3 per cent defect
Delivery	Less than 5 per cent late deliveries

Reference

Y. Akao (1991) *Hoshin Kanri: Policy Deployment for Successful TQM*. Cambridge, Massachusetts: Productivity Press.

Method 80   Is/is not matrix

Purpose

To identify patterns in observed characteristics by a structured form of stratification.

When to use

In teams, when trying to identify a problem precisely by organizing available knowledge and ideas about the problem. This is/is not matrix asks a series of questions that aim to pinpoint the problem, so guiding data collection.

Description of problem	Is (where, when, to what extent or to whom **does** it occur)	Is not (where, when etc. **does it not** occur when it could)	Therefore (what might explain the pattern)
Where (the location where it is noticed)			
When (the day, hour month or event: the relation to other events)			
What kind or how much (the type or category, degree, size)			
Who (Groups or individuals present or near the event)			

Figure 1   *Example of is/is not matrix*

Mysterious pains	Is	Is not	Therefore
Where	In fingers and legs, the pain appears symmetrical	In joints	Unlikely to be related to arthritis or rheumatism; unusual for physical problems to be symmetrical
When	Apparently random; sweating on palms of hand	Continuous	Brought on by events
What kind / how much	Shooting pains; goes on for variable time	Dull pain or ache	Not purely physical; could be stress related
Who	No patterns	Brought on by specific individuals	

Figure 2   *Is/is not matrix used in medical diagnosis*

How to use

The first step is to identify the problem, situation or idea to be analysed. Then ask a series of questions as given in Figure 1.

Benefits

This is/is not matrix allows the organization of knowledge and information in a structured format. This allows data collection to be guided by prior knowledge.

Example

A doctor is diagnosing a patient who has presented with mysterious pains in hands and legs. The doctor uses the is/is not matrix as a guide to diagnosis (Figure 2). The doctor concludes that the pains are stress related and confirms the diagnosis by taking the patient's blood pressure.

Reference

Charles H. Kepner and Benjamin B. Tregoe (1981) *The New Rational Manager*. Princeton, New Jersey: J.M. Publishing.

Method 81   Matrix data analysis

Purpose

To provide a picture of numerical data from a matrix diagram in an efficient way.

When to use

It can be used to obtain a picture of, for example, different products and market characteristics. It is an important means of analysing multi-variate data.

How to use

Its use is equivalent to principal component analysis which is a method of multi-variate statistical analysis. It requires some knowledge of statistical methods beyond the scope of this book.

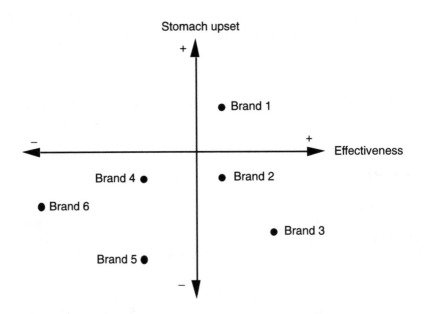

Figure 1   *Matrix data analysis*

Benefits

Helpful in analysing multi-variate data. It shows all the key data clearly and provides a schema of such things as different products and market characteristics.

Example

Figure 1 provides the results of an investigation into the effectiveness of different brands of aspirin. Brands 2 and 3 are effective and do not cause stomach upset, whereas Brand 1 is effective but causes stomach upset. Brands 4, 5, and 6 are not effective.

Reference

B. Bergman and B. Klefsjo (1994) *Quality: from Customer Needs to Customer Satisfaction.* New York: McGraw-Hill.

Method 82   Matrix diagram

Purpose

To provide information about the relationship and importance of task and method elements of the subject.

When to use

To organize and illustrate graphically the largest amount of data for the logical connection between various elements to show the importance of different relations by using graphic symbols.

How to use

The most commonly used matrix diagram is shown in quality function deployment (see Method 26).

Benefits

Simple method to show relationship between task and subject.

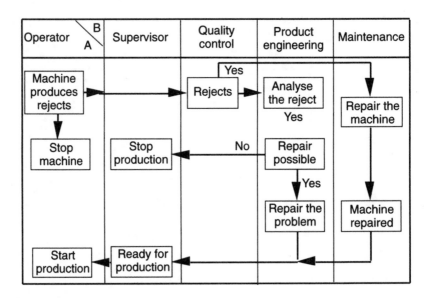

Figure 1   *Matrix diagram*

Example

Figure 1 demonstrates a matrix diagram in the situation where a machine is producing rejects.

Method 83   Moving average

Purpose

To identify trends in data when short-term variation or cyclical patterns are confusing the longer-term picture.

When to use

When monitoring a process to detect changes, or when a change has been made to process inputs to find out whether the process mean changes. Moving average charts can be used to monitor both variables and attributes data and are particularly useful for detecting long-term trends in data.

How to use

There are seven simple steps involved:

1   Collect the data. The type of data could be sales figures, factory volumes, error rate or exchange rate.
2   Decide which period to take the average over. If the data have a 13-week cycle, a 13-week period would be appropriate; if data are collected seven times a day, a moving average period of seven would be correct.
3   Accumulate the first seven figures (for a period of seven) and divide by seven. This is the first figure to be plotted.
4   Remove the first figure from the calculation, add in the next and again divide by seven.
5   Repeat step 4 until the data are all used.
6   Plot the data. The time sequence is usually plotted on the x axis, the moving average is plotted on the y axis.
7   Interpret the results.

Benefits

Moving average charts are relatively insensitive to short-term changes. This means that their main use is when you are trying to mask short-term variation in the process to highlight longer-term variations.

Example

A speciality treatment chemical refinery was examining factors affecting plant yield (Table 1). A moving average yield was plotted over a 52-week period. This involved 112 batches. The period of the moving average was four batches (see Figure 1).

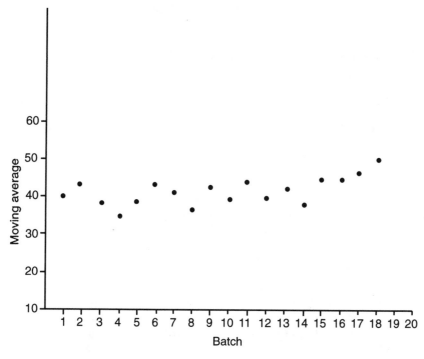

Figure 1 *Moving average chart*

Table 1 *Plant yield data in a chemical refinery*

Batch	Batch no.	Yield (%)	Sum	Mov. average
1	91001	35.0	35.0	*
2	91002	25.9	60.9	*
3	91005	53.5	114.4	*
4	91006	48.2	162.6	40.65
5	91009	46.6	174.2	43.55
6	91010	38.9	152.2	38.05
7	91014	42.1	140.8	35.20
112	91223	61.8	218.0	54.50

A plot of the raw data exhibits a large amount of local variation, making the picture very hard to see. The moving average damps this down, revealing the longer-term picture. There had been a step change in the yield at about week 32. This corresponded to a physical change in the way that the temperature was measured before the process was stopped. The result was that the process terminated at a lower temperature, so improving the yield.

Reference

R. Caulcutt (1995) *Achieving Quality Improvement*. London: Chapman and Hall.

Method 84   Multi-vari charts

Purpose

To show the dispersion in a process over the short and long term, using a graphic control chart.

When to use

It can be used during problem analysis to help isolate the cause of a problem and to understand the process when it is either stable or unstable.

How to use

1 Select the process and characteristics to be analysed and sampled internally.
2 Develop a method of recording the sample observations.
3 Collect the samples and record the values of the characteristics.
4 Plot each point on the chart and join the lowest point to the highest point with a straight line.
5 If the lines are of the same length and if they are in the same relative position then the process can be considered as stable. Otherwise there is an assignable cause.

Benefits

It helps to understand the variation in a process over the short and long term.

Example

Five parts were taken from a turning operation every 25 minutes. The diameter of each part was measured and plotted on the chart. A straight vertical line was drawn through each set of five points (Figure 1). In the multi-vari chart, the dispersion over the short time period is stable but the dispersion over the longer period looks suspicious. In this analysis, the length of the line describes the dispersion over a short period of time and the location of the lines indicates the dispersion over long periods of time.

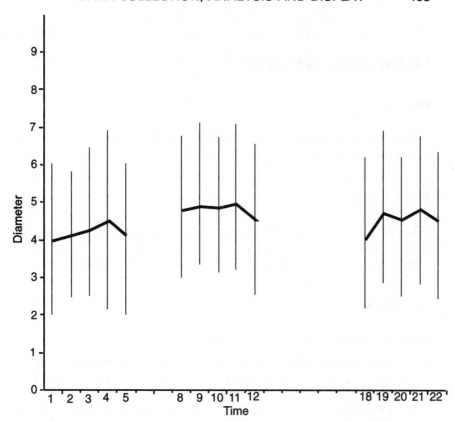

Figure 1   *Multi-vari chart*

Reference

Mario Perez-Wilson (1992) *Multivari Chart and Analysis: a Pre-experimentation Technique.* Scottsdale, Arizona: Advanced Systems Consultant.

Method 85   *NP* chart

Purpose

To identify when the number of defective items in a sample of constant size is changing over time.

When to use

When monitoring a process to detect changes, or when a change has been made to process inputs to find out whether the number of defective items also changes. NP charts are used when the sample size is constant.

How to use

There are seven simple steps involved:

1 Collect the data. Draw up a table showing the number of defective items for each lot number. The number of defective items is called *np*. The total number of lots is called *m*.
2 Plot the data from the table onto the *np* control chart (see Figure 1 on page 196). The successive lot numbers are shown on the horizontal axis, the number of defective units is shown on the vertical axis.
3 Calculate the central line as $n\bar{p} = \Sigma np/m$.
4 Calculate $\bar{p} = n\bar{p}/n$.
5 Calculate the control limits which are ± 3 s.d. about the central line and are calculated as:

$$\text{Upper control limit (UCL)} = n\bar{p} + 3\sqrt{n\bar{p}} \times \sqrt{(1-\bar{p})}$$
$$\text{Lower control limit (LCL)} = n\bar{p} - 3\sqrt{n\bar{p}} \times \sqrt{(1-\bar{p})}$$

If the lower control limit is less than zero it is taken to be zero.
6 Draw the central line and the control limits on the control chart.
7 Interpret the results.

Benefits

It can be difficult to separate out random variation (often called common cause or non-assignable variation) from real variation caused by changes to the process. *NP* charts are a way of doing this for the number of defective items with a sample size that is constant.

Example

A company is monitoring the number of defective bindings of a report. A binding is defective when the contents overlap the outer covers. A sample of 100 reports is taken on a daily basis and the figures are as follows:

Lot no.	Defective lapping (np)
1	5
2	6
3	5
4	4
5	2
6	1
7	2
8	0
9	2
10	3
11	4
12	3
13	4
14	3
15	2
16	3
17	2
18	4
19	3
20	2
Total	60

$$\text{Sample size} = 100$$
$$\Sigma np = 60$$
$$n\bar{p} = 60/20 = 3$$
$$\bar{p} = 3/100 = 0.03$$
$$3\sqrt{n\bar{p}} = 5.20$$
$$\sqrt{1-\bar{p}} = 0.985$$
$$3\sqrt{n\bar{p}} \times \sqrt{1-\bar{p}} = 5.12$$
$$\text{UCL} = 3 + 5.12 = 8.12$$
$$\text{LCL} = 3 - 5.12 = 0$$

The control chart shows that the process is under statistical control (Figure 1 on page 196).

Reference

Mal Owen (1989b) *SPC and Continuous Improvement*. London: IFS Publications.

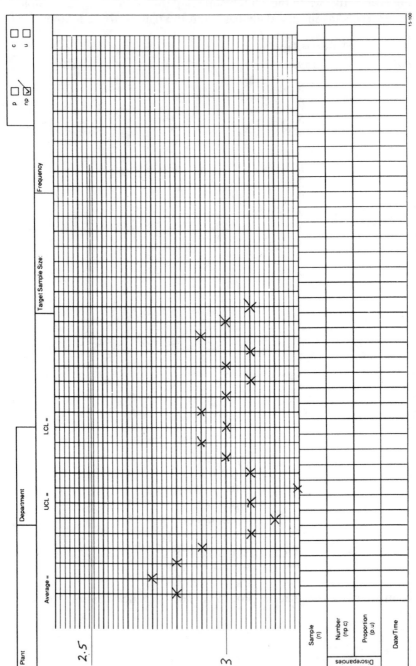

Figure 1 NP *chart*

Method 86   Paynter charts

Purpose

To display information over time in a way that allows changes in patterns of failure to be discovered. Paynter charts will show when one failure mode takes over from another in terms of importance or when the overall failure rate is changing over time.

When to use

When monitoring performance and setting priorities for improvement, Paynter charts can show changes in patterns of failure over time. They can also be used to record failures, errors or the occurrence of events that a team wishes to study and remedy.

How to use

The number of times an event occurs is shown on the vertical axis. The different time periods are shown on the horizontal axis. The occurrences are given in rank order with the highest first. The previous ranking is given for each occurrence. The total for each year is given in the extreme right-hand column.

Benefits

Paynter charts are able to display a large amount of data at one time, as opposed to having a different chart for each failure mode or occurrence. By displaying all the data together, a team is better able to see the total picture.

Example

Figure 1 shows a Paynter chart of the reasons for scrap in an automotive supplier. The horizontal axis shows changes month by month in the pattern. The ranking down the left-hand side of the chart shows changes in importance of the faults. It can be seen that, in the first month, 'No threads' became more prevalent. The Paynter chart also shows that 'Bad spray' is an increasingly important failure mode.

Previous ranking	Description	Jan.	Feb.	Mar.	Apr.	May	June	July	Aug.	Sept.	Oct.	Nov.	Dec.	Total
1	Others	1040	-	-	-	-	-	-	-	-	-	-	-	1040
2	Cockled gaskets	1006	-	-	-	-	-	-	-	-	-	-	-	1006
12	No threads	684	-	-	-	-	-	-	-	-	-	-	-	684
6	Bad spray	293	-	-	-	-	-	-	-	-	-	-	-	293
3	Dented bodies	283	-	-	-	-	-	-	-	-	-	-	-	283
7	Leaking seams	249	-	-	-	-	-	-	-	-	-	-	-	249
4	On-line bodies	205	-	-	-	-	-	-	-	-	-	-	-	205
5	Offset gaskets	186	-	-	-	-	-	-	-	-	-	-	-	186
8	Poor print	28	-	-	-	-	-	-	-	-	-	-	-	28
9	Eccentric assy.	12	-	-	-	-	-	-	-	-	-	-	-	12
14	Hole in body	4	-	-	-	-	-	-	-	-	-	-	-	4
15	Leaking welds	3	-	-	-	-	-	-	-	-	-	-	-	3
13	Off-sq. threads	-	-	-	-	-	-	-	-	-	-	-	-	-
10	Tight threads	-	-	-	-	-	-	-	-	-	-	-	-	-
11	Split b'plate	-	-	-	-	-	-	-	-	-	-	-	-	-
	Total scrap	3993	-	-	-	-	-	-	-	-	-	-	-	3993
	Total prod.	70 4783	-	-	-	-	-	-	-	-	-	-	-	70 4783

Figure 1 *Paynter chart*

Method 87   *P* chart

Purpose

To identify when the percentage of defective items in a sample of variable size is changing over time.

When to use

When monitoring a process to detect changes, or when a change has been made to process inputs to find out whether the percentage of defective items also changes. *P* charts are used when the sample size varies by more than $+$ 25 per cent of the mean sample size.

How to use

There are eight simple steps involved:

1   Collect the data. Draw up a table showing the number of defective items for each lot number (see Table 1). The number of defective items is called np. The sample size for each lot is called n. The total number of lots is called m.
2   For each lot, calculate the percentage defective $p\%$ by dividing np by n.
3   Plot the data from the table onto the p control chart. The successive lot numbers are shown on the horizontal axis, the percentage of defective units $p\%$ is shown on the vertical axis.
4   Calculate the $\bar{p}$. This is calculated as the sum of all the nps divided by the sum of all the ns and is written:

$$\bar{p} = \Sigma np / \Sigma n$$

5   Calculate the central line as $p \times 100\%$.
6   Calculate the control limits which are $\pm$ 3 s.d. about the central line and are different for each different value of n. They are calculated as:

$$\text{Upper control limit (UCL)} = \bar{p} + 3\sqrt{\bar{p}} \times \sqrt{(1-\bar{p})}/\sqrt{n}$$
$$\text{Lower control limit (LCL)} = \bar{p} - 3\sqrt{\bar{p}} \times \sqrt{(1-\bar{p})}/\sqrt{n}$$

If the lower control limit is less than zero it is taken to be zero.

7   Draw the central line and the control limits on the control chart.
8   Interpret the results.

Table 1 *Percentage of defective invoices*

Subgroup no.	Subgroup size	np	p%	UCL	LCL
1	19	7	37	62	0
2	20	8	40	40	0
3	8	2	25	79	0
4	13	1	8	68	0

UCL, upper control limit; LCL, lower control limit.

Benefits

It can be difficult to separate out random variation (often called common cause or non-assignable variation) from real variation caused by changes to the process. *P* charts are a way of doing this for the number of defective items with a sample size that varies by more than +25 per cent.

Example

An electrical distributor calculates a *P* chart for the percentage of defective invoices issued by its invoicing department. The figures are given in Table 1 and the control chart in Figure 1.

$$\Sigma n = 60$$
$$\bar{n} = 15$$
$$\Sigma np = 18$$
$$\bar{p} = 18/60 = 0.3$$

Reference

Mal Owen (1989b) *SPC and Continuous Improvement*. London: IFS Publications.

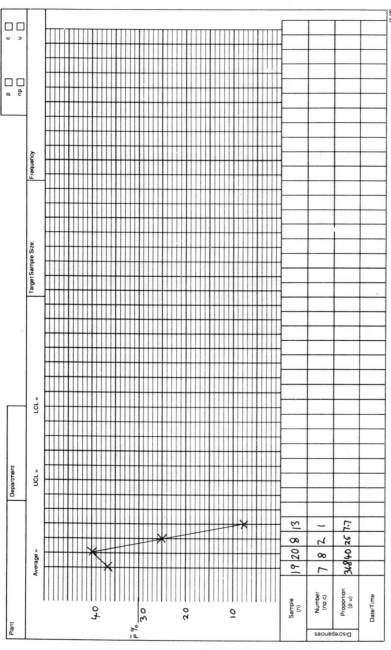

Figure 1 *P chart*

Method 88   Pie chart

Purpose

A way of pictorially representing data, pie charts are an effective means of showing the relative size of the individual parts to the total.

When to use

When you want to depict the relative size of individual parts to the total.

How to use

There are four simple steps in the calculation of a pie chart:

1   Collect the data and present in tabular form.
2   Total the data items and calculate the percentage of each item to the whole (the percentages when added up must equal 100 per cent).
3   Convert each percentage total into the relevant portion of the circle. Since a circle represents 360 degrees, each portion of data will occupy a slice of the whole. For example, a figure of 84.2 per cent of the whole is calculated to represent a portion of the circle as follows:

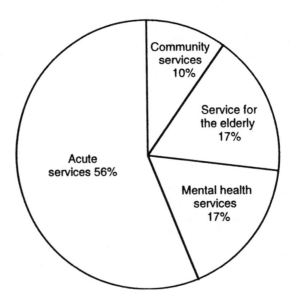

Figure 1   *Pie chart of health authority expenditure*

$$360° \times 84.2/100 = 303°$$

4 Draw the pie chart using a protractor to show the size of the slices within the pie.

Remember that the pie chart shows relative values. If you want to compare several pie charts, or if the size of the population changes, you must ensure that the relative value of all data is consistent for each.

Benefits

Pie charts give an easily understood picture that aids decision-taking.

Example

The following expenditure profile of a health authority is represented as a pie chart in Figure 1.

Acute services	£38.2M	55.4%	199°
Mental health services	£11.9M	17.2%	62°
Services for the elderly	£11.9M	17.2%	62°
Community services	£ 7.0M	10.2%	37°
Total	£69.0M	100%	360°

Method 89   Process analysis

Purpose

Enables a group to look for opportunities to improve processes. It can also be used to identify standards and measures for critical parts of processes.

When to use

A problem-solving team would use process analysis to discover gaps, dead ends or duplications in business processes and to show where improvements can be made.

How to use

This simple technique involves examining all the steps in a process and evaluating each of them critically.

1   Draw an outline flowchart of the process. This should be done by all members of the group who must be representative of the departments through which the process passes.
2   Each team member then draws a detailed flowchart for his or her own part of the process. This should then be agreed by other members of his or her department.
3   Analyse the flowcharts to look for dead ends, duplications and parts of the process that are missing. It is often neglected detail, such as standard instructions, that leads to excess process variability.
4   Plan to change the process according to the findings in 3.
5   Use the flowchart to identify what to measure and where to measure it. These measures can be fed back and used to improve the process.

Benefits

Often people in the same department believe that they are carrying out tasks in the same way but when the process is examined in detail it can be seen that there are critical differences.

An additional benefit is that many processes are not designed but develop with people's jobs. Frequently, no one challenges whether the process itself is still necessary or whether the steps give the best way to achieve the desired result.

Example

A company noticed that there was an apparently random problem with the dispatch of faulty products. This could not easily be traced to shifts, products or times. The problem-solving group drew an outline flowchart as shown in Figure 1 (on page 206). The two parts of the department then drew their detailed flowcharts for their own part of the process. The detailed flowchart for the second part is shown in Figure 2 (on page 207).

When the detailed information was collected, it became apparent that specifications were missing for key quality characteristics. This led to different operators interpreting the requirements in different ways and therefore the apparently random pattern. The group was able to put in place the missing information and the problem disappeared.

Reference

G. Born (1994) *Process Management to Quality Improvement.* New York: Wiley.

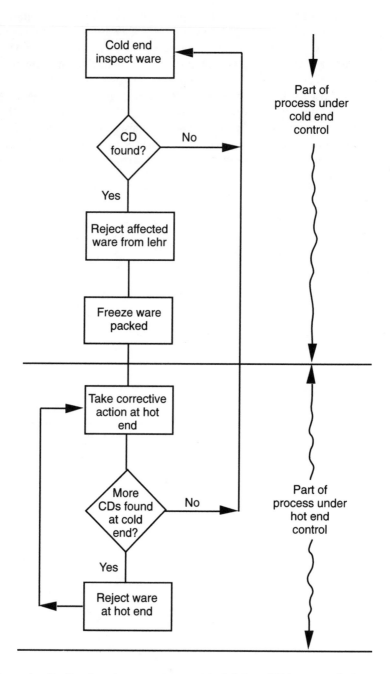

Figure 1   *Outline flowchart to prevent critical defects (CD) into packed ware*
Source: Kanji and Asher, 1993

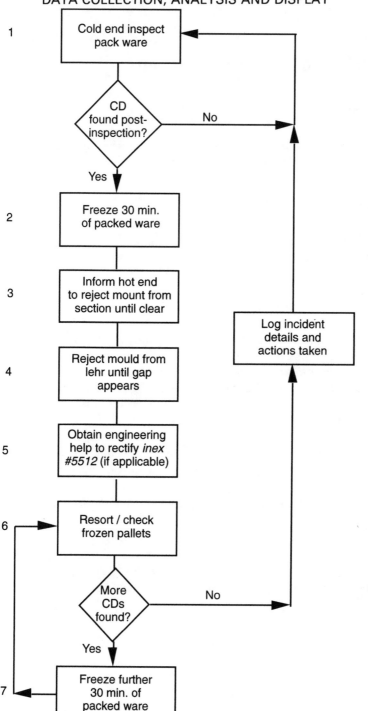

Figure 2 *Detailed flowchart (prevention of CDs into pack) of area under cold end control*

Source: Kanji and Asher, 1993

Method 90   Process capability

Purpose

To demonstrate whether a process is capable of meeting a specification and to calculate an index to show this capability.

When to use

During design, commissioning or post-commissioning to demonstrate the capability of a product or process.

How to use

The calculation of process capability depends on whether the process is measured in terms of variables data or attributes data.

For *variables data*, capability is expressed in terms of an index called Cp. Cp is dependent upon the actual centre of the process performance being the same as the centre of the specification. When this is so, the index is calculated as:

$$Cp = \frac{\text{Total specification width}}{\text{Total process spread}}$$

where the total process spread is estimated using the formula

$$\text{Total process spread} = 6 \times \bar{R}/d_2$$

where $\bar{R}$ is the mean of the ranges (see Method 69) and d_2 is a statistical constant depending upon the same size as shown below.

n	d_2
2	1.128
3	1.693
4	2.059
5	2.326

Various values of Cp, together with the parts per million (ppm) of items produced above specification, are as follows:

Cp	ppm
1.00	1350
1.33	32
1.67	0.3
2.00	0.001

For *attributes data*, the capability of the process is often called the first run capability (FRC) and is calculated as:

$$\text{FRC} = (1-\bar{p}) \times 100\%$$

where $\bar{p}$ is the percentage of defective items (see Method 87).

Benefits

By establishing the facts about process performance it becomes easier for technical, marketing and manufacturing departments to talk to each other, and for companies to talk to their customers and suppliers.

Example

During the manufacture of glass bottles, the internal diameter of the bottle neck is a critical parameter. The specification of the neck is agreed with customers as 1.5 cm ± 0.01 cm. The total specification spread is therefore 0.02cm.

Based upon a set of samples of size 5, the mean of the ranges $\bar{R}$ was 0.0075 cm. Total process spread was calculated as $6 \times \bar{R}/d_2 = 0.019$. The capability was therefore $0.02/019 = 1.035$. Using the figures given above, it can be seen that approximately 1350 ppm are being produced out of specification.

Reference

Mal Owens (1989) *SPC and Business Improvement*. London: IFS Publications.

Method 91   Sampling

Purpose

A method by which a small number of items (the sample) is drawn from a larger number of items (the population) in order to draw a conclusion about the population based upon information from the sample.

When to use

Sampling is used when the overall size of the population is such that to gain full information would be impossible, time-consuming or very costly. Under some circumstances, sampling can be more accurate than information obtained from the total population.

How to use

There are five common methods of sampling in common usage.

Random sampling

This is when the sample is designed so that every member of the population has an equal probability of being chosen. It is usual to do this using random numbers to tell you which items to select. Random sampling is used when there are no known patterns or trends in the data.

The disadvantages are that it can be costly and that, if the population is ill defined, it is impossible to number the items to allow the sample to be designed.

Stratified sampling

This is when the sample is designed to reflect prior knowledge about the population. An example of this is social trends where groups A, B, C, D and E are chosen. A random sample is then taken within each group or stratum. Stratified sampling gives more precise information than random sampling.

Cluster sampling

This is when the population is split into groups or clusters and then a random choice of clusters is made. Random sampling then takes place within the cluster.

An example of this is the use of opinion polls to predict the outcome of an election by picking polling stations and then carrying out a random sample of those leaving the polling station.

Systematic sampling

This is simply when the population is believed to be randomly spread and a sample of 1 in *n* is taken. An example would be taking a sample of students by taking every fifth student from the list of names.

Quota sampling

This is a form of stratified sampling where those taking the sample are given a quota to fulfil. They interview everyone fitting the quota until the quota is complete. This is common in market research where people have to interview so many mothers with children etc.

Whichever method of sampling is used, the process to be followed is the same:

1 Define the population from which the sample is to be taken. This is the most difficult step. Most problems resulting from sampling are caused by lack of clarity at this stage.
2 Define the sampling technique. This may be already known from information on the population.
3 Define the sample size.
4 Take the sample.

Benefits

Sampling is a faster process than using the whole population due to the smaller amounts of data being collected. It is also cheaper because less time is used. It can be more accurate and have a known degree of accuracy.

Example

As part of the diagnostic phase of a total quality process, an organization used stratified sampling to determine how many employees to interview to find representative views of quality problems in the organization.

Reference

M.R. Beauregard, R.J. Mikulak and B.A. Olson (1992) *A Practical Guide to Statistical Process Improvement*. Amsterdan: Van Nostrand Reinhold.

Method 92   Scatter diagrams

Purpose

To allow the relationship between cause and effect to be established.

When to use

Scatter diagrams are used when a group is trying to test whether a relationship exists between two items – often a cause and effect.

How to use

There are four simple stages to draw a scatter diagram:

1 Collect data about the causes and effects.
2 Draw the cause on the horizontal axis.
3 Draw the effect on the vertical axis.
4 Draw the scatter diagram.

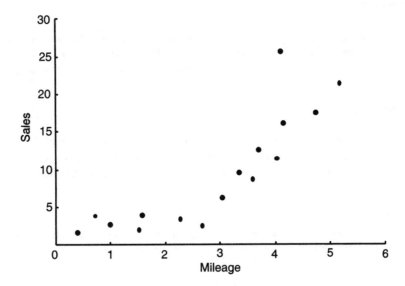

Figure 1   *Scatter diagram*

Benefits

Scatter diagrams help to bring the facts to bear when discussing problems. They help to reduce the amount of 'gut feeling' involved with the problem-solving.

A word of caution. Just because there appears to be a relationship, it does not mean that one thing causes another; the relationship might be fortuitous or through a third, unknown, variable. If a relationship appears to have been found, proof must be sought.

Example

A team is examining the relationship between the mileage of salesmen and the volume of business sold. Mileage, the cause, is plotted along the horizontal axis and sales per annum, the effect, are plotted along the vertical axis. The scatter diagram shows a clear relationship between mileage and sales (Figure 1).

Reference

P. Lyonnet (1992) *Tools of Total Quality*. London: Chapman and Hall.

Method 93   Spider web diagrams

Purpose

To show performance against a target when several criteria are being set.

When to use

When team members need motivation to achieve results that they might previously have believed were impossible, one way to do this is to show how their performance compares with the best achievable. Spider web (or arachnoid) diagrams give a very visible way of showing progress and performance against several targets at the same time.

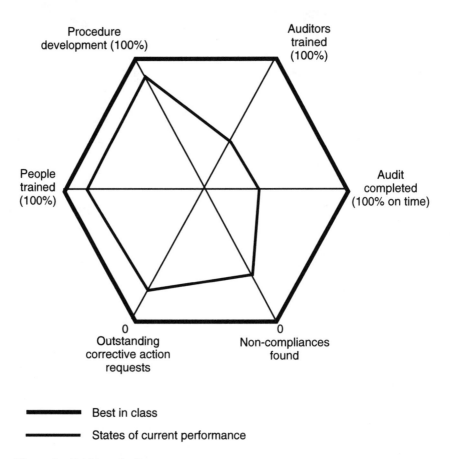

Figure 1   *Spider web diagram*

How to use

For each of the parameters or targets involved, identify a precise definition of the target and how it can be measured. Measure the performance against the target and display it on the diagram. Each time the performance is measured a new diagram is constructed.

Benefits

The spider web diagram shows at a glance how progress is being made towards targets. When benchmarking, the spider web diagram can be used to show current performance, the immediate aim, the average in class or the overall best in class performance.

Example

A company decided to use the spider web diagram to show the development of its quality system against the target set (Figure 1). The parameters and measures chosen were:

- procedure development: % developed on time
- internal auditors trained: % against target
- internal audits completed: % against target
- non-compliances found: total number
- corrective action requests outstanding: number
- people trained in the system: % against target.

Method 94   Statistical process control (SPC)

Purpose

To identify when processes are changing over time.

When to use

When monitoring a process to detect changes, or when a change has been made to process input to find out whether the process output changes. Statistical process control (SPC) can be used for manufacturing and service processes, using the flowchart of the process as a basis.

How to use

There are eight simple steps involved:

1   Identify the process to be studied.
2   Draw an outline flowchart of the process.
3   Draw a detailed flowchart of the process.
4   Using the flowchart, decide which data to collect.
5   Using tally charts or concentration diagrams, collect the data.
6   Analyse the data using histograms or other techniques to ensure that the data are suitable for control charting.
7   When necessary, use problem-solving techniques, such as Pareto analysis and cause and effect analysis, to remove special cause variation from the process.
8   Draw the data on a control chart.

There are two basic types of data:

1   *Variables data*   when the characteristic being measured is continuously variable over a range of values. This might be temperature, weight, output, time to process a form.
2   *Attributes data*   when the characteristic being measured has one of two values. This might be on/off, present/absent, go/no go. Attributes data comes in two forms:
    • *defective units*: for example, forms with errors, deliveries with faults etc.
    • *Defects*: for example, errors in forms where there can be more than one error per form, faults in shipments where shipments can have several errors.

Benefits

It can be difficult to separate out random variation (often called common cause or non-assignable variation) from real variation caused by changes to the process. Control charts allow decisions to be made about processes on the basis of fact rather than gut feeling.

Example

Figure 1 (on page 218) shows how to select the correct type of control chart according to type of data and sample size.

Reference

J.S. Oakland and R.F. Followell (1990) *Statistical Process Control*. London: Butterworth/ Heinemann.

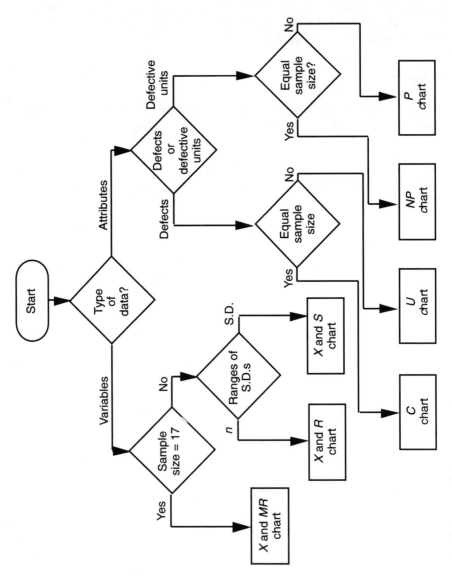

Figure 1 *Choosing the right control chart*

Method 95   Stem and leaf diagram

Purpose

To present raw data and to show their distribution visually.

When to use

As a tool in exploratory data analysis such as histograms. It is useful for illustrating large amounts of data.

How to use

Round numerical data to the number of tens by trimming off the last digits. In Figure 1 the ascending order of the data is 3, 5, 6, 7, 7, 8, 8, 9 . . . 33, 35. The last digit of each observation is called a leaf and the other digits form a stem. For an observation of 35, the leaf is 5 and the stem is 3.

Benefits

1   A stem and leaf diagram sideways provides a histogram of the data with numerical values.
2   The method can be modified to suit different data.
3   Quartiles, i.e. Q_1, Q_2 etc. can be read directly.
4   The diagram gives a useful five-number summary, i.e. lower quartile, median, upper quartile, the smallest and the target value.

Tens	Units	Total
0	3	1
0	5 6 7 7 7 8 8 9	8
1	0 1 1 2 2 3 3 3 4 4	10 ➔ Q1
1	5 5 5 6 6 7 7 7 8 8 8 9 9	13 ➔ Q2
2	0 1 1 2 3 3	6 ➔ Q3
2	5 5 7 8 8 9 9	7
3	0 1 2 3	4
3	5	1
Stem	Leaf	50

Figure 1   *Stem and leaf diagram*

Example

A stem and leaf diagram is given in Figure 1. The stem in this case is the tens and to the right are the units. The top value is thus 3 and the bottom value is 35. The diagram sideways also provides a histogram with the numerical values and Q_1, Q_2 and Q_3.

Reference

B. Bergman and B. Klefsjo (1994) *Quality: from Customer Needs to Customer Satisfaction.* New York: McGraw-Hill.

Method 96   Tally charts

Purpose

To collect data when the value of a defect or problem is important.

When to use

Either during problem definition when you are collecting data to find out what is happening, or when you have implemented a solution and you are collecting data to monitor the new situation.

How to use

There are five simple steps to draw a tally chart:

1 Agree the data to be collected. This step is vital: you cannot analyse data that have not been collected.
2 Design the tally chart.

Type of call	Tally	Frequency
Stationery	ЖЖ IIII	9
I've done it wrong	ЖЖ IIII	9
How do I ......?	ЖЖ ЖЖ I	11
Soft crash	ЖЖ I	6
Other soft	ЖЖ	5
Can I have ......?	ЖЖ	5
Code numbers	ЖЖ ЖЖ III	13
Hardware	III	3
Other int.	ЖЖ I	6
Other ext.	IIII	4
Total		71

Figure 1   *Tally chart analysis of telephone calls*

3   Test the chart using someone who has not been involved in the design. Get him or her to use the chart without assistance. If necessary, modify the chart.
4   Design a master tally chart. If more than one person is to be involved in data collection, you will need to bring together all the data collected. The way to do this is to use a master chart.
5   Collect the data.

Benefits

By establishing the facts about the value of failures, a team can plan to identify the causes of failure and look for ways of removing them. Actions are taken on the basis of evidence, not feeling.

Tally charts are an excellent way of involving people in all areas in quality improvement. They provide a simple method of data collection that can be easily understood and applied in office and work areas. Often, there are simple ways to draw tally charts without asking people to record the results. Marbles or golf balls can be used to record events very simply.

Example

The tally chart shown in Figure 1 represents the results of an analysis of calls to a company's computer help desk. The data were used to assist in the design of induction training.

Method 97   Tree diagrams

Purpose

To identify the tasks and methods needed to solve a problem and reach a goal.

When to use

When you want to break down vaguely formulated customer wishes about a product into customer requirements on a manageable level, or to investigate all possible aspects of customer wishes that present a problem. Tree diagrams can be used to develop short-term goals before finalizing long-term goals.

How to use

Build a 'tree' systematically from a statement of a goal through headings to 'branches' of plans and action. Trees are best developed as a team. General issues are subdivided into specific issues. A particular use of this structure is that of a 'fault tree' where the tree structure is used in a cause and effect fashion to analyse causes of faults.

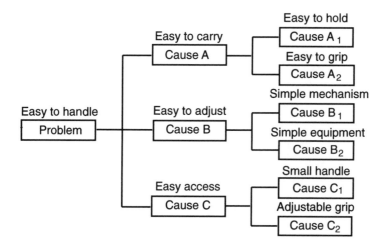

Figure 1   *Tree diagram*

Benefits

To solve a complicated problem and to achieve the desired goal in a systematic way.

Example

With the aid of a tree diagram, a company is seeking to design equipment that is easy to handle (Figure 1).

Reference

B. Bergman and B. Klefsjo (1994) *Quality: from Customer Needs to Customer Satisfaction.* New York: McGraw-Hill.

Method 98   *U* chart

Purpose

To identify when the number of defects in a sample of variable size is changing over time. The *U* chart could be used to monitor errors in typing, errors on drawings, marks in materials.

When to use

When monitoring a process to detect changes or, when a change has been made to process inputs, to find out whether the number of defects also changes. *U* charts are used when the sample size varies by more than + 25 per cent of the mean sample size.

How to use

There are seven simple steps involved:

1 Collect the data. Draw up a table showing the number of defects for each lot number. The number of defects is called *C*. The sample size for each lot is called *n*. The total number of lots is called *m*.
2 For each lot, calculate the number of defects per unit *U* by dividing *C* by *n*.
3 Plot the data from the table onto the *U* control chart. The successive lot numbers are shown on the horizontal axis, the number of defects per unit *U* is shown on the vertical axis.
4 Calculate the centre line $\bar{U}$. This is calculated as the sum of all the *C*s, divided by the sum of all the *n*s and is written as

$$U = \Sigma C\, /\, \Sigma n$$

5 Calculate the control limits. The control limits are ± 3 s.d. about the central line and are different for each different value of *n*. They are calculated as

$$\text{Upper control limit (UCL)} = \bar{U} + 3\sqrt{\bar{U}}/\sqrt{n}$$
$$\text{Lower control limit (LCL)} = \bar{U} - 3\sqrt{\bar{U}}/\sqrt{n}$$

If the lower control limit is less than zero it is taken to be zero.
6 Draw the central line and the control limits on the control chart.
7 Interpret the results.

Table 1 *Report sheet errors*

Date	Shift	No. sheets n	No. errors c	Errors/sheet w
3/5	6 × 2	3	6	2.00
	2 × 10	3	4	1.33
4/5	6 × 2	3	5	1.66
	2 × 10	1	3	3.00
6/5	6 × 2	1	0	0
9/5	6 × 2	3	6	2.00
	2 × 10	3	8	2.66
10/5	6 × 2	3	1	0.66
	2 × 10	3	3	1.00
11/5	6 × 2	3	4	1.33
	2 × 10	3	2	0.67
12/5	6 × 2	3	2	0.67
13/5	6 × 2	1	1	1.00
16/5	6 × 2	3	1	0.33
	2 × 10	3	0	0
17/5	6 × 2	3	3	1.00
	2 × 10	2	6	2.00
18/5	6 × 2	3	2	0.67
	2 × 10	3	3	1.00
19/5	6 × 2	3	2	0.67
	2 × 10	2	1	0.50
20/5	6 × 2	3	3	1.00
Total		22	58	$\Sigma C = 66$

Benefits

It can be difficult to separate out random variation (often called common cause or non-assignable variation) from real variation caused by changes to the process. U charts are a way of doing this for the number of defects with a sample size that varies by more than +25 per cent.

Example

For data on report sheet errors see Table 1. The resulting U chart is given in Figure 1.

$$\text{CL} = \bar{U} = \frac{\Sigma C}{\Sigma n} = \frac{66}{58} = 1.14$$
$$K = 3\sqrt{U} = 3.2$$
$$\text{upper control limit} = \bar{U} + \frac{K}{\sqrt{n}}$$
$$\text{lower control limit} = \bar{U} - \frac{K}{\sqrt{n}}$$

Reference

T.P. Ryan (1989) *Statistical Methods for Quality Improvement*. New York: Wiley Interscience.

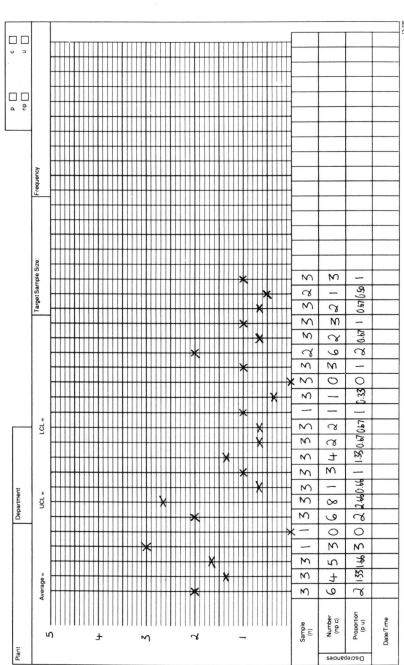

Figure 1 *U chart*

Method 99   *X* moving range (*X-MR*) chart

Purpose

To identify when a value is changing over time.

When to use

When monitoring a process to detect changes, or when a change has been made to process inputs to find out whether the mean value changes. *X* moving range is used to monitor variables data, when the values can vary over a continuous range, and when the sample size at each sampling point is 1. This, for example is the case with monthly sales figures, when there is only one figure, production figures or when the cost of taking the measurement is very high.

How to use

There are six simple steps involved:

1 Collect the data. Draw up a table showing the readings for each of the samples at each lot. The number of samples in each lot is 1. The total number of lots is called *m*.
2 For each lot calculate the moving range by subtracting the *X* value from the previous *X* value. There is no moving range for the first *X* value.
3 Working down the table, add together all the *X* values and divide the result by the number of lots *m*. This value is the grand mean and is written $\bar{X}$ (called *X* bar). Again, working down the table, add together all the moving range values and divide by *m*−1. This value is written *MR*.
4 Calculate the control limits for the *X-MR* chart using the formula:

$$\text{Upper control limit (UCL)} = \bar{X} + 3 \times MR/d_2$$
$$\text{Lower control limit (LCL)} = \bar{X} - 3 \times MR/d_2$$

d_2 is a constant that when multiplied by 3*MR* gives 3 s.d. for the *X-MR* chart.
5 Plot the data from the table onto the *X-MR* control chart. The successive lot numbers are shown on the horizontal axis; the *X* values are shown on the vertical axis.
6 Interpret the results.

Benefits

It can be difficult to separate out random variation (often called common cause or non-assignable variation) from real variation caused by changes to

Table 1 *Time to achieve less than 5mbar pressure*

Shift letter	Cast no.	Time to <5 mbar	Moving range
C	1	9.0	–
A	2	5.5	3.5
A	3	7.0	1.5
A	4	7.5	0.5
A	5	7.0	0.5
B	6	8.0	1.0
B	7	6.5	1.5
B	8	6.0	0.5
B	9	6.5	0.5
C	10	9.0	2.5
C	11	8.0	1.0
C	12	9.5	0.5
C	13	9.0	0.5
D	14	6.5	2.5
D	15	5.5	1.0
D	16	6.0	0.5
D	17	7.5	1.5
D	18	7.5	0
D	19	9.0	2.5
A	20	9.5	0.5
A	21	9.0	0.5
A	22	8.0	1:0
A	23	10.5	1.5
A	24	8.5	2.0
B	25	11.0	2.5
B	26	7.5	3.5

the process. *X-MR* charts are a way of doing this for variables data with a sample size that is 1.

Example

The time to achieve a pressure is shown for 26 successive production runs (Table 1). Since there is only one such time on each production run, the *X-MR* chart is the appropriate way to control this process (Figure 1 on page 230).

$$m = 26$$
$$\Sigma X = 204.5; \bar{X} = \Sigma X/m = 7.9$$
$$\Sigma R = 34.5; \bar{R} = \Sigma R/(m-1) = 1.38$$
For $n = 2$; $d_2 = 1.128$, therefore $3.\bar{R}/d_2 = 3.67$
$$UCL = \bar{X} \div 3 . \bar{R}/d_2 = 11.53$$
$$LCL = \bar{X} - 3 . \bar{R}/d_2 = 4.19$$

Reference

R. Caulcutt (1995) *Achieving Quality Improvement*. London: Chapman and Hall.

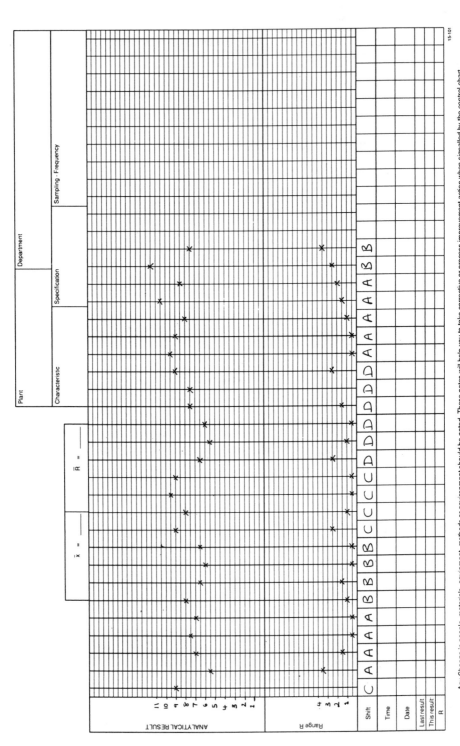

Figure 1   X-MR chart

Any Change in people, materials, equipment, methods or environment should be noted. These notes will help you to take corrective or process improvement action when signalled by the control chart.

Method 100 $\bar{X}$-R chart

Purpose

To identify when the mean value or range in a sample of constant size is changing over time.

When to use

When monitoring a process to detect changes, or when a change has been made to process inputs to find out whether the mean or range changes. $\bar{X}$-R charts are used to monitor variables data, when the values can vary over a continuous range, and when the sample size at each sampling point is greater than 1.

Examples of data drawn on an $\bar{X}$-R chart include time to process insurance claims, temperature of a chemical reaction and width of metal slabs.

How to use

There are seven simple steps involved:

1 Collect the data. Draw up a table showing the readings for each of the samples at each sampling point. The number of samples at each sampling point is called n. The total number of sampling points is called m.
2 For each sample, calculate the mean $\bar{X}$ by adding together the X values and dividing by the sample size n. For each sample, calculate the range by subtracting the smallest value in each sample from the largest. This value is called R.
3 Working down the table, add together all the $\bar{X}$ values and divide the result by the number of sampling points m. This value is the grand mean and is written $\bar{\bar{X}}$ (called X bar bar). Again, working down the table, add together all the R values and divide by m. This value is written $\bar{R}$ and called R bar.
4 Calculate the control limits for the $\bar{X}$ chart using the formula:

$$\text{Upper control limit (UCL)} = \bar{\bar{X}} + A_2 \times R$$
$$\text{Lower control limit (LCL)} = \bar{\bar{X}} - A_2 \times R$$

   A_2 is a constant, that when multiplied by R, gives 3 s.d. for the X chart.
5 Calculate the control limits for the R chart using the formula:

$$\text{Upper control limit (UCL)} = D_4 \times R$$

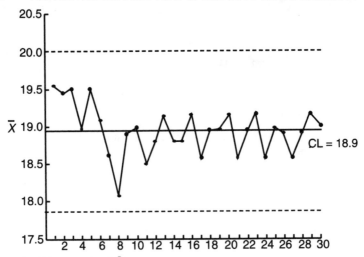

Figure 1   *Line graph of X̄*

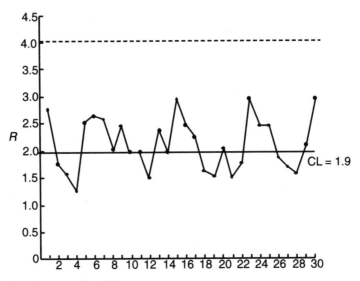

Figure 2   *Line graph of* R

$$\text{Lower control limit (LCL)} = D_3 \times R$$

D_4 and D_3 are statistical constants that give $\pm$ 3 s.d. for the R chart. These limits are not symmetrical about the central line R.

6   Plot the data from the table onto the $\bar{X}$-R control chart. The successive sampling points are shown on the horizontal axis, the $\bar{X}$ and R values are shown on the horizontal axis. Conventionally, the R chart is plotted below the $\bar{X}$ chart.

7   Interpret the results.

Table 1 *Data used to monitor thickness of machined parts*

Lot no.	1 X_1		2 X_2		3 X_3		4 X_4		5 X_5	Sum ΣX	Mean $\bar{X}$	Range R
1	21.0	+	18.9	+	19.8	+	19.7	+	18.2	97.6	19.52	2.8
2	19.8	+	19.9	+	19.1	+	20.0	+	18.2	97.0	19.40	1.8
3	20.0	+	19.2	+	19.5	+	20.2	+	18.6	97.5	19.50	1.6
4	19.5	+	18.6	+	19.9	+	19.7	+	19.8	97.5	19.50	1.3
5	20.5	+	18.0	+	18.8	+	18.6	+	18.6	94.5	18.90	2.5
6	20.8	+	18.1	+	19.0	+	20.1	+	19.5	97.5	19.50	2.7
•	•									•	•	•
•	•									•	•	•
•	•									•	•	•
29	18.1	+	20.2	+	20.2	+	18.4	+	18.8	95.7	19.14	2.1
30	20.9	+	19.2	+	18.0	+	18.4	+	18.3	94.8	18.96	2.9
Total											567.0	57.0
Mean											18.9	1.9

Benefit

It can be difficult to separate out random variation (often called common cause or non-assignable variation) from real variation caused by changes to the process. $\bar{X}$-R charts are a way of doing this for the variables data with a sample size that is greater than 1.

Example

Figures 1 and 2 show the use of an $\bar{X}$-R chart to monitor the thickness of machined parts using the data given in Table 1. The number of sampling points $m = 30$; the size of each sample $n = 5$.

$$m = 30 \quad n = 5$$
$$\bar{R} = \frac{\Sigma R}{m} = \frac{57}{30} = 1.9$$
$$\bar{\bar{X}} = \frac{\Sigma \bar{X}}{m} = \frac{567}{30} = 18.9$$
$$UCL_R = D_4\bar{R} = 2.11 \times 1.9 = 4$$
$$LCL_R = D_3\bar{R} = 0 \times 1.9 = 0$$
$$A_2\bar{R} = 0.58 \times 1.9 = 1.1$$
$$UCL_X = \bar{\bar{X}} + A_2\bar{R} = 18.9 + 1.1 = 20$$
$$LCL_X = \bar{\bar{X}} - A_2\bar{R} = 18.9 - 1.1 = 17.8$$

Reference

J.S. Oakland and R.F. Followell (1994) *Statistical Process Control*. London: Butterworth/Heinemann.

REFERENCES

Akao, Y. (1991) *Hoshin Kanri: Policy Deployment for Successful TQM*. Cambridge Massachusetts: Productivity Press.

Amsden, D.M., Butler, H.E. and Amsden, R.T. (1991) *SPC Simplified for Services*. London: Chapman and Hall.

Anderson, D.R., Sweeney, D.J. and Williams, T.A. (1994) *An Introduction to Management Sciences*. New York: West.

Barker, Thomas D. (1994) *Quality by Experimental Design*. New York: Marcel Dekker.

Beauregard, M.R., Mikulak, R.J. and Olson, B.A. (1992) *A Practical Guide to Statistical Process Improvement*. Amsterdam: Van Nostrand Reinhold.

Bell, D., McBride, P. and Wilson, G. (1994) *Managing Quality*. London: Butterworth/Heinemann.

Bergman, B. and Klefsjo, B. (1994) *Quality: from Customer Needs to Customer Satisfaction*. New York: McGraw-Hill.

de Bono, Edward (1970) *Lateral Thinking*. New York: Harper and Row.

Born, G. (1994) *Process Management to Quality Improvement*. New York: Wiley.

Bossert, J.L. (1991) *Quality Function Deployment: a Practitioner's Approach*. Milwaukee: ASQC Quality Press.

Bourner, T., Martin, V. and Race, P. (1993) *Workshops that Work*. New York: McGraw-Hill.

Buzan, T. (1974) *Use your Head*. London: Ariel Books.

Camp, R.C. (1989) *Benchmarking: the Search for Industry Best Practices that lead to Superior Performance*. Milwaukee: ASQC Press.

Caulcutt, R. (1995) *Achieving Quality Improvement*. London: Chapman and Hall.

Chang, R. and Niedzwiecki, M. (1993) *Continuous Improvement Tools*. California: Richard Chang.

Cook, Sarah (1992) *Customer Care*. New York: Kogan Page.

Crosby, P.B. (1979) *Quality is Free*. New York: McGraw-Hill.

Crosby, P.B. (1984) *Quality without Tears*. New York: McGraw-Hill.

Dahlgaard, J.J., Kanji, G.K. and Krisjensen, K. (1990) 'A comparative study of quality control methods and principles in Japan, Korea and Denmark', *Total Quality Management*, 1: 115–32.

Dale, B.G. and Plunkett, J.J. (1991) *Quality Costing*. London: Chapman and Hall.

Day, R.G. (1993) *Quality Function Deployment: Linking a Company with its Customer*. Milwaukee: ASQC Quality Press.

Deming, W.E. (1986) *Out of the Crisis*. Cambridge, Massachusetts: MIT Press.

Fordyce, J.K. and Weil, R. (1978) *Managing with People*. New York: Addison-Wesley.

Gibbs, Lance. (1987) 'Tools for problem solving'. London: PA Consulting Group (internal report).

Hutchins, D. (1985) *Quality Circles Handbook*. London: Pitman.

Imai, M. (1986) *Kaizen: the Key to Japan's Competitive Success*. New York: Random House.

Ishikawa, Kaoru (1985) *Guide to Quality Control*. Tokyo: Asian Productivity Press.

John, P.W.M. (1990) *Statistical Methods in Engineering and Quality Assurance*. New York: Wiley.

Kane, Victor E. (1989) *Defect Prevention*. New York: Marcel Dekker.

Kanji, G.K. (1993) *100 Statistical Tests*. London: Sage.

Kanji, G.K. and Asher, M. (1993) *Total Quality Management Process: a Systematic Approach*. Oxford: Carfax.

Karlof, B. and Ostblom, S. (1994) *Benchmarking: a Signpost to Excellence in Quality and Productivity*. New York: Wiley.

Kepner, C.H. and Tregoe, B.B. (1981) *The New Rational Manager*. Princeton, New Jersey: J.M. Publishing.

Kume, H. (1985) *Statistical Methods for Quality Improvement*. Tokyo: AOTS.

Logothetis, N. and Wynn, H. (1991) *Quality through Design*. Oxford: Oxford Science Publications.

Lyonnet, P. (1992) *Tools of Total Quality*. London: Chapman and Hall.

McAndrew, G. and O'Sullivan, S. (1993) *FMEAs: a Manager's Handbook*. London: Stanley Thornes.

Nakajima, Seiichi (1988) *Introduction to TPM*. Cambridge, Massachusetts: Productivity Press.

Oakland, J.S. and Followell, R.F. (1990) *Statistical Process Control*. London: Butterworth Heinemann.

Onnies, A. (1992) *The Language of Total Quality*. Castellamonte, Italy: T Pok Publication on Quality.

Owen, M. (1989) *SPC and Business Improvement*. London: IFS Publications.

Parker, G.W. (1992) *Achieving Cost Efficient Quality*. London: Gower.

Perez-Wilson, Mario (1992) *Multivari Chart and Analysis: a Pre-experimentation Technique*. Scottsdale, Arizona: Advanced Systems Consultant.

Ross, P.J. (1988) *Taguchi Techniques for Quality Engineering*. New York: McGraw-Hill.

Ryan, T.P. (1989) *Statistical Methods for Quality Improvement*. New York: Wiley Interscience.

Spenley, P. (1992) *World Class Performance through Total Quality*. London: Chapman and Hall.

Tukey, J. (1991) *Exploratory Data Analysis*. New York: Addison-Wesley.

INDEX